CAPE PLAYS

The Joker of Seville

&

O Babylon!

by the same author

In a Green Night: Poems 1948–60
Selected Poems
The Castaway
The Gulf and Other Poems
Dream on Monkey Mountain and Other Plays
Another Life
Sea Grapes

For Ralph and Dody Thompson

Contents

The Joker of Seville

3

O Babylon!

155

The Joker of Seville

For Ronald Bryden

Note

This play is my first attempt to adapt the work of any author, ancient or contemporary, and what I hope I have drawn from the original—Tirso de Molina's *El Burlador de Sevilla*—is primarily the pace of its scenes and its meter. I have no Spanish whatsoever and was never in awe of the archaic or heraldic tongue that Tirso's language may be, but as with most romance languages, one can be swept along in a narrow torrent of powerful lyricism, without comprehension, propelled by the passion of its sound. On such a rapid journey, the plot, like the landscape, rushes past and blurs detail; cribs or translations serve as a map, but the language is my own.

It may have been this element and nothing more which suggested to Ronald Bryden, the literary adviser of the Royal Shakespeare Company, that a West Indian poet, living in a country whose language and music have one form, should attempt this adaptation. Yet, without knowing Tirso's speech, I felt a contemporary, provincial, and immediate enthusiasm for his play, because of Trinidad. The wit, panache, the swift or boisterous élan of his period, and of the people in his play, are as alive to me as the flair and flourishes of Trinidadian music and its public character.

I began laboriously by trying to translate into alternating rhymes of eight-foot lines directly from the old Spanish, but soon gave up. What I surrendered, having read once through Roy Campbell's mainly blank-verse translation, was the exactness of vocabulary, but what I hope I have kept is the rhyme scheme and tempo. The most significant thing for me was to feel that I could adapt such a complete work without any sense of artifice. If I were living in another culture, I might have felt I was indulging in a purely literary exercise. But the verse play is not a literary exercise in the West Indies. It is not necessary here to go into the inherent dramatic narrative of the calypso or to redescribe the necessity of physical enactment of folk chants. Tirso's play is not only about a man who must have come from the folk imagination and the formal religion of his Spaniards, but it also contains their musical life and the validity of their rhetorical style. One can hear in his verse the cry of flamenco and the pulse of the guitar. Once its music entered my head, there was no artifice in relating the music and drama of the Spanish verse to what strongly survives in Spanish Trinidad, or, debased as critics may think it, to the thrum and cry of the parang, in which, with typical Spanish duality, the song of praise has the same pitch as the lament.

Legends find new vessels. When one oracle is exhausted, they may spring up in unexpected ground, just as vital, real, vulgar, and apprehensible as they were when they first sprang to life. The more I worked on this play, the closer I got to a feeling for the Spanish-creole life in Trinidad.

D.W.

Characters

RAFAEL, *an old actor*
DON JUAN TENORIO, *a knight*
OCTAVIO, *a knight*
RIPIO, *Octavio's servant*
CATALINION, *Juan's servant, a Moor*
ISABELLA, *Duchess of Naples*
DON PEDRO, *Juan's uncle, ambassador to Naples*
THE KING OF NAPLES
THE KING OF CASTILE
DON GONZALO DE ULLOA, *a commander*
ANA DE ULLOA, *his daughter*
DON DIEGO TENORIO, *Juan's father*
TISBEA, *a fishergirl of New Spain*
ANFRISO, *a fisherman, her betrothed*
CORYDON, *a fisherman*
THE MARQUIS DE MOTA, *a knight*
BATRICIO, *a farmer*
AMINTA, *Batricio's betrothed*

In Rafael's troupe: ACE OF DEATH; QUEEN OF HEARTS; JOKER; JACK, *a boy*

Chorus representing GUARDS, A SHIP'S CREW, WEDDING GUESTS, NUNS, COURTIERS, LADIES, SLAVES, FISHERGIRLS, MUSICIANS, WHORES, STICKFIGHTERS, DANCERS

The action, preferably staged in the round, takes place in a stickfight arena in the Trinidad countryside, then moves to seventeenth-century Spain, on All Souls' Eve. The play is in two acts.

For arena staging, the only large unit required is a mobile ornamented box which serves as a sarcophagus, a bed, a table, and a fountain. The audience should sit on wooden bleachers close to the action, as in a rural bullfight, cockfight, or stickfight. The orchestra should be visible.

This play, based on Tirso de Molina's *El Burlador de Sevilla*, was commissioned by the Royal Shakespeare Company, with whose permission the Trinidad Theatre Workshop first performed it at the Little Carib Theatre, Port of Spain, Trinidad, on November 28, 1974, with music by Galt MacDermot, lighting by John Andrews, and directed by the author, with the following cast:

RAFAEL	Hamilton Parris
JUAN	Nigel Scott
OCTAVIO	Syd Skipper
RIPIO	Ivor Picou
CATALINION	Errol Jones
ISABELLA	Helen Camps
DON PEDRO	Anthony Hall
THE KING OF NAPLES	Hamilton Parris
THE KING OF CASTILE	Lawrence Goldstraw
DON GONZALO	Stanley Marshall
ANA	Joy Ryan
DON DIEGO	Albert LeVeau
TISBEA	Stephnie King
ANFRISO	Winston Goddard
CORYDON	Henry Daniel
DE MOTA	Terry Jones
BATRICIO	Errol Pilgrim
AMINTA	Norline Metivier
DUENNA	Avis Martin
ABBESS	Ermine Wright
ACE OF DEATH	Andrew Beddeau
QUEEN OF HEARTS	Adele Bynoe
JACK	Brenda Hughes

Alternates: Albert LeVeau (Juan); Carol La Chapelle (Ana), Stephnie King (Jack), Brenda Hughes (Tisbea)

Dancers: Carol La Chapelle, Noble Douglas, Norline Metivier, Allison Guerra. Choreographers: Carol La Chapelle, Noble Douglas

Musicians: June Nathaniel (piano), Patrick Flores (guitar), Everard Flores (drums), Ken Brathwaite (cuatro), Henry Miller (bass), Nelson Villafana (flute), Richard Reid (cuatro). Musical Director: June Nathaniel

Act One

With a painted paradise at the end of it . . .
    EZRA POUND, *Pisan Cantos*

PROLOGUE

Dusk. A field, ringed with bleachers, used as a bull ring, a cockpit, or stickfighters' gayelle, on a Caribbean estate. Nearby, a village cemetery with fresh wreaths and lit candles with a statue of DON GONZALO. *Opposite: the village cathedral.* RAFAEL, *the village elder, enters in a costume resembling the statue's. In the distance, a procession of candles held by a chorus of villagers.*

CHORUS
> *Sevilla, a voces me llama*
> *El Burlador, y el mayor*
> *gusto que en mi puede haber*
> *es burlar una mujer*
> *y dejarla sin honor,*
> *y dejarla sin honor.*

(*The villagers enter and assume the postures of statues*)

Act 1 / Prologue THE JOKER OF SEVILLE

RAFAEL

This is the eve of All Souls,
our carnival of candles,
when our village, San Juan, re-creates
a legend that cannot grow old.
You New Andalusian estates,
Valencia, moonlit Aranquez,
whose oceans of sugar cane thresh
in the night wind, bring him across
the ocean, with salt, real flesh
as man, to live his loves over.
   (*Kneels*)
Earth, who holds him like a lover,
release him to us for one night,

(DON JUAN *appears, the villagers stir into life*)

that, with candles like fireflies on
this night of his resurrection,
we stickmen can challenge our champion,
the greatest stickman: Don Juan!

(*Cheering. Stick play. The women circle* JUAN)

JUAN

   (*Sings*)
Sevilla gave me the honor
of calling me Don Juan, the Joker,
and it's true what I do may undo a
woman, but I renew her
and honor her with dishonor.

(RAFAEL *presents his troupe: the* ACE OF DEATH, *the* QUEEN OF HEARTS, *the* JOKER, *the* JACK)

RAFAEL
>(Sings)
>Now of all the cards in the pack,
>Ace, King, Queen, Joker, and Jack,
>of all the royal cards in the pack,
>Ace, King, Queen, Joker, and Jack,
>The Ace is the dead man, of course,
>but the Joker is really the boss;
>he can change to elation each grave situation,
>sans humanité!

CHORUS
>He can change to elation each grave situation,
>sans humanité!

ACE OF DEATH
>Now this word: "sans humanité,"
>is "without pity," that's what it mean;
>this word: "sans humanité,"
>is without pity, that's what it mean.
>If you chant that response to me,
>and shout it without pity,
>you go start off the action, to our satisfaction.

(JUAN exits)

CHORUS
>Sans humanité!
>You go start off the action, to our satisfaction,
>sans humanité!

RAFAEL
>O dim, majestical time,
>teach our bodies to move in rhyme.

Act 1 / Prologue   THE JOKER OF SEVILLE

Again, majestical time,
bring shimmering Naples to mind.
Tell the stars over old Seville,
when we kill, we don't really kill.
Look, our swords are all sticks and our duels just stickplay,
sans humanité!

STICKFIGHTERS

Our swords are all sticks and our duels just stickplay,
sans humanité!

RAFAEL

And now, as our play begin,
see Isabella undressing.
In Naples, where we begin,
see Isabella undressing.
She was to play with Octavio in bed,
but she draw the Joker instead.
When she blow out the candle, she start off the scandal,
san humanité!

CHORUS

(Departing)
When she blow out the candle, she start off the scandal,
sans humanité!

(All exit)

SCENE 1

Naples, night. A street near the palace. ISABELLA, DUENNA, *and* GUARDS *in a bedroom above.* OCTAVIO *enters, in soldier's cloak;* RIPIO *carrying a priest's robe.*

OCTAVIO
> Ripio, the whole thing's laughable!
> By next month, I'm to be married,
> but she's locked in that impregnable
> fortress. Do they think lovers heed
> the law? There, look! She's signed the air
> twice with her candle, so near dawn,
> when all those stars, like sentries, tire
> of fighting sleep. With this robe on,
> I'll play Isabel's confessor.

RIPIO
> Well, you blaspheme for a great cause.

(*They laugh.* JUAN, *disguised as a crone emerges from the shadows*)

JUAN
> Aren't you the Duke Octavio, sir?

OCTAVIO
> Yes.

JUAN
> And this soldier's cloak is yours?
> My dead husband had one. Your Grace,
> all Naples knows that warrior

Act 1 / Scene 1   THE JOKER OF SEVILLE

who'll be Duchess Isabella's
husband; but pray God she'll never
be widowed like me, sir; after
he died, doing a soldier's work,
with wind whipping off the harbor
like a knife, and not even his cloak
to shield her.

OCTAVIO

              Tonight, this one will.

(OCTAVIO *gives him his cloak*)

JUAN

It's All Souls'. I'll light a candle
for you and Mistress Isabel
in the cathedral.

(JUAN *moves off*)

RIPIO

              Incredible!
If we meet another beggar,
you'll be naked.

OCTAVIO

              No, watching her,
I pitied women.
  (*Shouts*)
              Candlelight
kindle your faith, love! May my cloak's
arms husband you through this cold night.

(OCTAVIO *and* RIPIO *exit*)

JUAN
>And God help you . . .
>>(*As himself*)
>>>If you hate jokes!

(*Music:* CATALINION *enters, helps* JUAN *to change into* OCTAVIO's *cloak.* JUAN *climbs the stairs into* ISABELLA's *room, past* GUARDS)

CATALINION
>(*Sings*)
>*By the shimmering harbor of Naples,*
>*its waters embroidered with light,*
>*my master, Don Juan Tenorio,*
>*moves under the mantle of night.*

(*The bedroom.* JUAN *as* OCTAVIO. ISABELLA *greets him*)

ISABELLA
>Octavio, you've come.

JUAN
>>Not yet, love.

CATALINION
>*When my master fights, both sides surrender,*
>*and wrestle their fury to bliss,*
>*and the fiercer the fighting, the surer*
>*their mutual victory is.*
>
>*It's my job to stand by with these horses,*
>*I'm his servant Catalinion,*
>*and since duels are worse than divorces,*
>*just watch the conqueror run.*

Act 1 / Scene 1

ISABELLA
  Octavio?

JUAN
      Yes, love?

ISABELLA
      Let this lamp
  light both our faces to recall
  our joy.

(JUAN *leaps up*)
JUAN
      Lady, turn on that lamp,
  and you've lit your own funeral!

ISABELLA
  That voice! You're not Octavio!
  His cloak . . . Who are you? Turn your head!

JUAN
  I'm nobody, that's all you know;
  my name is Nobody, or you're dead!

(ISABELLA *screams. Two* GUARDS *run on with torches and pikes*)

JUAN
  Stop! I'm the Duke Octavio!
  One at a time! Are you crazy?
  You're common soldiers, don't you know
  that by the rules of chivalry
  you fight a duke by ranks? Who's first?

(DON PEDRO *enters, sword drawn*)

THE JOKER OF SEVILLE

Act 1 / Scene 1

DON PEDRO
>Don Pedro Tenorio, you carbuncle!
>A duke of Spain, so, do your worst!

(*He charges* JUAN. *They grapple*)

JUAN
>It's Juan, Don Pedro. You're my uncle.

DON PEDRO
>(*Shouts*)
>*Juan!*

(JUAN *lunges*)

JUAN
>Two! Three! Four!

DON PEDRO
>   I'll lose my job—
>Seville's ambassador to Naples.
>Think of the cannonading cables
>exchanging governmental wrath
>that will be hurtled back and forth!
>Breathe heavily, give the illusion
>that we're in dire combat; when
>I fall and cry, "Help, gentlemen!"
>you can take off in the confusion.
> (*Shouts*)
>Iberian dog!
> (*Whispers*)
>   There's a vessel
>pointed for Lisbon at flood tide.

Act 1 / Scene 1 THE JOKER OF SEVILLE

She's not much, but she's the best you'll
get now, so forget your pride
and take her! Now, just draw some blood.
Why am I doing this, do you know?

JUAN

Because you too were once a stud.
There!

(JUAN *lunges*. DON PEDRO *falls*)

DON PEDRO

     I'm dying! Duke Octavio
killed me!
    (JUAN *exits. The* GUARDS *chase him.* DON PEDRO *rises, stops them*)
Wait, wait, you fools! The villain's flight,
by the strict code of chivalry,
is secondary to the right
I have, before my last good night,
to make my dying speech! The swan
before he finds the glittering reach
and silver margin, where the reeds
bend in the moaning zephyrs, finds
the strength to utter his last note,
so I, to this phlegmatic throat . . .
summon this music . . .

(*The* KING OF NAPLES *enters*)

KING OF NAPLES
Don Pedro!

THE JOKER OF SEVILLE

GUARD
   Sir, he's dying.

KING OF NAPLES
      Speak, old friend.
 (*To the* GUARD)
Coward! Liar! This man's not hurt.

GUARD
 He's a duke. He says he's dying.
 I'm simply saying what I heard.

DON PEDRO
 He's right. It's my wound that's lying.
 It's less important than its gape
 proclaims. Sorry.

(ISABELLA *approaches.* GUARDS *exit*)

KING OF NAPLES
     You'll be sorrier
for who did this. Did he escape?
Did she go with him?

ISABELLA
    I'm here.

KING OF NAPLES
 And far too visible. Duchess,
 draw your loose gown, and smooth your hair.
 That calm face contradicts your dress.

ISABELLA
   Your servant and your mirror, sir.
   If you see lechery in my face,
   you see all nature. There you are.

KING OF NAPLES
   You've made a brothel of this place.
   You and . . . Don Pedro, who was he?

DON PEDRO
   The Duke Octavio, sir. He's
   ridden off with his servant, Ripio.

ISABELLA
   It was not Octavio.

DON PEDRO
                  He said so
   himself.

KING OF NAPLES
          If not Octavio,
   the man that you would have married,
   then God save him from someone who . . .

ISABELLA
   It was nobody, my lord.

KING OF NAPLES
   . . . has the devotion of a whore.

THE JOKER OF SEVILLE   Act 1 / Scene 1

ISABELLA
  I am not that, my lord.

KING OF NAPLES
                    Woman,
  I heard their hooves hammering across
  the palace courtyard, ringing fire!
  Each hoofbeat nails you to a cross
  of lifelong penance. Isabella,
  your ecstasy will be remorse.
  One year in a cold convent cell
  should whip that flesh free of desire
  and damn that galloping duke, half-horse,
  half-devil, who rode you to Hell.

ISABELLA
  It was not . . .

KING OF NAPLES
            You hear me, woman?

ISABELLA
  A woman, yes! That was my wrong,
  born to this privilege of debasement,
  ordered to keep a civil tongue
  locked in its civil ivory casement.
  When you are pious, she's a wife,
  and, when appropriate, a whore.
  Now that you've simplified my life
  to silence, I will speak no more.

(*Silence*)

19

Act 1 / Scene 1 THE JOKER OF SEVILLE

KING OF NAPLES
>From fire to ice! If your contempt
is prayer, pray that your hot-heeled duke,
when you're freezing in the Convent
of Barefoot Nuns, ducks my rebuke,
because under chivalric law
his penalty is silence too:
death, for desecrating honor!
That honor isn't owned by you
or me, it is the law of God.
Remove her shoes and take her off.

(Exit with DON PEDRO. NUNS and an ABBESS enter. A chant begins as ISABELLA is undressed, then robed as a nun)

NUNS
 (Sing)
*Brevis est amor
in nostra vita.
Certis est dolor,
sed in te, Mater,
in te, Sancta soror,
crescit felicitas.*

(JUAN and CATALINION enter below. JUAN sings to the ABBESS as ISABELLA and NUNS pass in procession)

JUAN
 (Sings)
*O brave fat lady, waiting to get laid,
go, spread this gospel to those in your charge:
teach them that righteous beauty is betrayed,
not by false men, but by that lecher, Age.
Age that will rope their delicate calves with blue,*

20

that'll cloud their April eye with rheum and mist;
that shall do unto them as it did you;
tell them to hear its thunder in their wrist:
tell them that far-off drumbeat counts their doom,
that round their turreted breasts it has set siege,
till wrinkles like inaccurate archers come,
and its lewd agonies riddle every womb.
Duenna, say it happens not to some,
but to them all, you keeper of their keys!

(*The* NUNS, DUENNA, *and* ISABELLA *exit*)

SCENE 2

The same. CATALINION *restrains* JUAN.

CATALINION
>You're mad. Let's go, sir! Why circle
>right back here when we could have gone?

JUAN
>To hide in the open; a skill
>I learned from the chameleon:
>Keep still and some hot idiot
>will come pelting to you and wheeze:
>"Sir, did you see a man about
>your age, height, the same color eyes?"

(DON PEDRO *runs up*)

Act 1 / Scene 2 THE JOKER OF SEVILLE

DON PEDRO
> Tell me, sir, did you see a man,
> about your size, almost your height?
> What are you still doing here, Juan?
> Your ship's sailing any minute!

JUAN
> Now I've seen what they do to her!
> I knew they'd punish her with God.
> She marries Him and saves their honor.
> Give this cloak to Octavio! He'll
> be dressed like a priest. There he is!

(JUAN *and* CATALINION *exit as* OCTAVIO *and* RIPIO *enter,* OCTAVIO *in a priest's robe and cowl*)

DON PEDRO
> Good God!
>   (*Hides cloak*)
>   Stop, Father! You'll be killed!
> I risked my career to do this.

OCTAVIO
> Killed? Why, my son?

DON PEDRO
>   "Your son?" Exiled
> at least then, Father. Leave Naples!
> I know you're Duke Octavio
> under that cowl; better stay there! Please!
> Octavio's nobody now.

(OCTAVIO *lifts his hood*)

THE JOKER OF SEVILLE   Act 1 / Scene 2

OCTAVIO
　　All right, then. Let's begin again.

DON PEDRO
　　You're Duke Octavio? Correct?

OCTAVIO
　　Yes.

DON PEDRO
　　　　I'm ambassador from Spain?

OCTAVIO
　　They say to Spain's profound regret.

DON PEDRO
　　Don't joke! This is a thing for tears!
　　You have cuckolded yourself, sir!

OCTAVIO
　　Not yet.

DON PEDRO
　　　　　　They say you stealthily
　　claimed what was yours; bit earlier
　　than is the custom. 'Tisn't for me
　　to judge these things, but there you are!
　　Your love, Duchess Isabella,
　　fell victim to a seducer
　　disguised as you.

OCTAVIO
　　　　　　　　What?

Act 1 / Scene 2 THE JOKER OF SEVILLE

DON PEDRO
>   The fellow
> shouted out boldly as he fled:
> "Tell them it's Duke Octavio!"
> I shouldn't be standing here. I'm dead.
> You killed me.

OCTAVIO
>   Did the King say so?
> Exile? Well, I'd have used this robe
> to blaspheme past the palace guards
> as her confessor, so this rape
> is a more cruel joke of God's.
> But couldn't anyone capture
> him? One man! He ran, and that's it?

DON PEDRO
> Pelted, you mean! That predator,
> nimbler than any marmoset,
> skittered around every corner,
> then turns and bites me! You can bet
> that the astonished palace guards
> think you're a marvelous acrobat.

OCTAVIO
> And Isabella?

DON PEDRO
>   She's now God's.
> She's condemned to one year's exile
> in a convent. Run, I beg you!

OCTAVIO

    I have to think a little while!
    Sorry, Don Pedro. I thank you,
    but as a man I start to doubt
    that there wasn't some sort of plan
    between them. How could she have not
    distinguished us? I know you've risked
    your job, sir. You'd better be gone.
    You've no clue at all who did this?

DON PEDRO

    None! Well, I've a nephew named Juan
    back in Seville, thank God, who is
    so pious that sometimes I rage
    at virtue. Know him?

OCTAVIO

                We've not met.

DON PEDRO

    You must. He sends you this message,
    but anger makes people forget;
    he said he'd like to thank you for
    this soldier's cloak. There, sir, you see?
    There're grateful men left in this world.

(DON PEDRO *gives* OCTAVIO *the cloak, then exits.* OCTAVIO *laughs*)

RIPIO

    Before you swear revenge, hear me!
    Sir, if they've made her God's bride now,

isn't your vengeance blasphemy?
Your honor an adulterer's vow?
She's one of all this world's women.

OCTAVIO

She is a fire that consumes all,
and that's Octavio's madness, friend.
Even if Hell rise and Heaven fall,
the world, but not my love, will end.
Go, Ripio.
   (RIPIO *exits*)
             Now, my joke begins,
let him decline deeper from grace.
When he can't distinguish his sins
from jokes, then I will show my face.
   (*He cowls himself*)
There's an old abbey on a hill
named for the Moor, Saint Benedict.
I'll pray to let my hatred heal
there, because of God's interdict
against revenge. In the passing
of one year, then, my mind will know
if to rid earth of such a thing
serves God's will, not just the law.
(*Exits*)

SCENE 3

The Spanish court. COURTIERS, LADIES, DON DIEGO, DON GONZALO, ANA. *Then the* KING OF CASTILE.

KING OF CASTILE

Ah, Don Gonzalo! Welcome home
to Seville! We've missed you at court,
you, and your daughter Ana's charm.
   (ANA *is presented, withdraws*)
Seville has heard such great report
about Lisbon, her jealousy's
aroused and it must be appeased.

GONZALO

Sir, Lisbon, named for Ulysses
Ulissibona, was baptized
correctly. He once said his name
was Nobody. They named it well,
because Lisbon, for all its fame,
is nobody next to Seville.
   (*Laughter*)
Twelve iron gates unlock their view
of the river Guadalquivir,
that links Seville with silver through
olive groves whose emeralds are
enough to wet a jeweler's eye.
It was for this broad-backed river
sirens divorced the sea. Their song
calls the homeless wanderer here:
Trojans, who would forget the wrong

Act 1 / Scene 3   THE JOKER OF SEVILLE

    done Troy, and Babylonians,
    what the great Hanging Gardens were.
    Like Troy and Babylon at once
    soars our invincible Alcazar!
    When Jupiter was drizzling gold,
    his reign fell here: this Hall of Kings,
    with beams so high, they cannot hold
    within the vision of a lynx.
    Yet what praise this Alcazar brings
    Seville, Seville returns it all
    humbly to Christ, the King of Kings,
    by her majestic cathedral
    that in the eye of paradise
    is nothing, as diminished as
    our glory in that lynx's eyes.
    And yet, your Majesty, all this
    could be simply interpreted
    as boasting, if all that it did
    was to extol our treasuries.
    Seville is rich only if she,
    like my own daughter, still obeys
    God, King, and Father. Let me be
    grateful and generous in my praise
    of her. For her to lose her faith,
    her dowry of virginity,
    to venal pride is to court death.
    Traveling from Lisbon, sir, I've come
    into this wisdom. I have seen
    that our great treasures are at home.

KING OF CASTILE
    May they remain as they have been.
    You, Don Gonzalo de Ulloa,

I make my personal chamberlain;
you have been a marriage broker
between great Portugal and Spain,
so let two human halves cohere
in marriage now, by my command.
There's a fine, vigorous chevalier
to whom I give your daughter's hand:
a young and supple-tempered blade,
Juan Tenorio, Diego's son,
now on that rigorous crusade
in our dominions overseas
which God our Heavenly Father's given,
to bring the New World to our knees
for a new earth, and a new heaven,
to kiss this cross, the sword of Christ.

(ANA *kneels.* DON GONZALO *is invested*)

DON DIEGO
Your Majesty, my son is blest.

GONZALO
My daughter, Ana, is honored.
But, sir, if we could for just
one minute be alone . . . My head
is reeling . . .

(*The* KING OF CASTILE *gestures, the court leaves.* DON DIEGO, ANA *support* GONZALO)

KING OF CASTILE
        You're gray as stone.
Speak to us now. Nobody's here.

Act 1 / Scene 3   THE JOKER OF SEVILLE

GONZALO
  Nobody?

ANA
    Father, we're alone.

GONZALO
  My heart is galloping with fear!
  I saw two horsemen cloaked in mist
  on a vague ridge above Lisbon;
  then the fog swirled into a fist
  that wrote on air: "Gonzalo, one
  of these will murder you!" Then
  I saw VENGEANCE carved in stone
  on my own tomb. Look, there! Horsemen!

(*Music. All freeze;* JUAN *and* CATALINION *enter, riding*)

JUAN
   (Sings)
  They don't know who I was before,
  but they guess who I am, after;
  but before they are sure, and require more,
  I leave them, limp with laughter.
  For once around is ground enough
  for any virgin's pleasing,
  so she can give to her true love
  with appetite increasing.
  His love is trusting, true, and his
  the shoulder which she cries on,
  but all her tears are for what disappears
  with me on the horizon.

KING OF CASTILE
>These visions mean nothing at all.
>They're the penalty of old wounds.
>Come, sir. Is this the man men call
>the Terror of the Moors? Thousands
>of those heathen fell to your name:
>Commander of Calatrava.

DON DIEGO
>Who can predict death from a dream?

ANA
>How could there have been riders here?

KING OF CASTILE
>Your daughter will be marrying
>Don Diego's son. Go in, you're tired.

GONZALO
>I feel as if I'm carrying
>a statue of myself inside
>my flesh. You're right. I'll go to bed.

KING OF CASTILE
>Care for him. Your father's the pride
>of all Seville. For that, Seville
>will make you its loveliest bride.

ANA
>Sir, it's yours and my father's will.

(ANA, GONZALO *exit, then* DON DIEGO *and the* KING OF CASTILE. JUAN *and* CATALINION *dismount*)

Act 1 / Scene 3   THE JOKER OF SEVILLE

JUAN

　The port of Lisbon. The last shore,
　Catalinion, before we're free
　for the New World. Free, from that bore
　with the fog beard! The sea! The sea!

(Music: A sail with a cross is hoisted. JUAN leads off the horses as a gang of chained SLAVES, CAPTAIN and CREW come on deck. CATALINION sings)

CATALINION

　El Capitán was a quaking wreck,
　el first mate muy borracho,
　los crew, who staggered round the deck,
　didn't know arse from elbow.
　　(A dance begins with CAPTAIN, MATE, CREW, and SLAVES)
　El cargo was a reeking lot
　of Negroes, coon and bimbo,
　who screamed the blues, when they were not
　up practicing el limbo.
　　(SLAVES do a limbo dance, and are beaten. CATALINION begins
　　to undress. The sea gets rough)
　But they said, when we said: "It's more
　to us like cries of anguish . . ."

CAPTAIN and CREW

　(Sing)
　Theese ees a Spaneesh sheep, señor,
　and they do not speak Spanish!

CAPTAIN

　(Sings)
　Out of great suffering, we know,
　they make their songs and dances.

*These galley slaves who learn to row
in time will bless their chances.
Listen:*

SLAVES

(Sing)
*Hey, hey, hey!
Is the U.S.A.
Once we get dere,
we gonna be O.K.!*

CATALINION

*And if you asked where you were going,
the first mate would get frantic,
repeating any question with:*

FIRST MATE

(Sings)
¿Quién sabe? The Atlantic!

(*A storm begins*)

CATALINION

*They say Columbus find this place
by accident, he lucky!
Same accident in our case,
every slave drown, except me.*

SLAVES

*Hey, hey, hey!
Is the U.S.A.
Once we get dere,
we gonna be O.K.!*

CATALINION

I am the one slave to survive
this shipwreck with my master.
But I'm not sure, now I'm alive,
which is the worse disaster.

   (*A loud wave. Shipwreck.* JUAN, *almost naked, nearly drowned, climbs onto* CATALINION's *back*)

For this new world, its promised feasts,
is nothing but the old one,
as long as men are beasts, and beasts
still bear their master's burden.

SLAVES

Hey, hey, hey!
Is the U.S.A.
Once we get dere,
we gonna be O.K.!

(JUAN *and* CATALINION *collapse on the beach. The sea subsides; morning. Paradisal light. Music.* TISBEA, *a fishergirl of mixed blood, enters with a basket*)

SCENE 4

TISBEA

O what is more refreshing than this image of a sun-browned fishergirl with literary pretensions descending through the golden almond leaves, past the lecherous, gummed eyes of old trees bulging with amazement like those who watched Helen walk the battlements of Troy, even though books are hard to come by, and for me, Tisbea, to be that image? Yes, for this doe-eyed creature to come to this beach necklaced with the wreckage of a storm! This image would startle the world, O breasts forever firm in their principles! O little lipped door always locked to lechers! O plump inviolate little heart! I must remember to take all this down; every day I lose three metaphors through laziness! Yet if I were Nausicaä and there, sprawled on the crumpled satin of the beach at Tarragon . . . oh, that's too good, too good, I must remember it, no quill, no quill . . . What was it—if I were Nausicaä on the smooth beach, no, not smooth, was it smooth? Well, anyway, and there lying naked and sleek . . . Why did I bring up Nausicaä . . . I am not Nausicaä, that shell-gathering princess, I am humble Tisbea on the wrecked coast of New Tarragon and I am simply going to walk along this beach singing my innocent song when I encounter . . .

(*Screams*)

A man! Naked!

Two men! One black!

Shipwrecked.

Go back!

(*Music*)
(*Sings*)

If from the darts of Cupid's bow,
I, Tisbea, am immune,
still bright is my unblemished brow
as the unblemished moon.
Do I flee
from the sight
of such naked, impending
doom? Is it right

Act 1 / Scene 4   THE JOKER OF SEVILLE

that I see
what I see, depending
before me.
As I stand here, divided
between mercy and
modesty, should my stand
be one-sided?
Can truth be so naked?
Where are all of those vows
that I just prided
myself on?
Go! Stay! says a little voice.
How's that? Another
little voice sings on!
Breasts, why are you heaving?
Heart, why do you beat?
Tiny feet,
aren't you leaving?
I must go, I must!
Oh, the tempest that's seething
in me, I shall burst!
See the heave of this bosom.
O dark heat in this bust,
O wonderful morning,
can this be lust?

JUAN
    (Coughing)
The shipwrecked Ulysses, broken by the loud sperm?—loud spume!—heaved on the breast of ocean, was not luckier than when through salt-seared eyes he saw dawn-nimbused Nausicaä . . .

TISBEA
> Oh, sir, you know Homer?

JUAN
> Is there anyone else? Pardon me, but as I lay there, me and my shipwrecked servant, who I'll introduce when he's fully clothed . . . may I borrow that basket to contain my immodesty? Thank you.
> (TISBEA *extends the basket. He wears it*)
> Could not help admiring, even in my spent condition, your rounded, beautifully pointed syntax. I have never overheard, or heard for that matter, any woman, duchess, or eunuch speak as eloquently, and I have heard many, and now I'm quite exhausted and must lie down. Somehow.

(*He lies down.* CATALINION *tries to rise, but* JUAN *forces him back into the sand*)

JUAN
> Down, slave! And keep your fish hidden from this lovely naiad.

TISBEA
> You speak well, sir, for someone who's just been shipwrecked. I had no idea that you were overhearing what I was saying to myself. But you need succor like Narcissus, and I stand here talking.

JUAN
> And I lie, standing.
> (*The conversation between* TISBEA *and* JUAN *is conducted obliquely, with* JUAN *half under a basket and* CATALINION *face down*)
> Tell me, fair sea nymph, where is this?

Act 1 / Scene 4 THE JOKER OF SEVILLE

TISBEA

The coast of New Tarragon.

JUAN

(*Shouting*)
O God, forgive me, forgive me, great Neptune!

(CATALINION *sits up and ducks back down.* TISBEA *kneels*)

TISBEA

Where hurting you? Sir, what wrong?
(*Pause*)
Are you in agony, sir?

JUAN

(*Holding her*)
I shall never be forgiven. Never!

TISBEA

For what? It's not a pain, then?

JUAN

No, it is simply, Oh, I can hardly bear it! And I shall only say it if you seal these berry-bright salt lips, and seal up in that vault, your high-principled breast, what rape of chivalry this prince has done . . .

TISBEA

A prince? I promise, your Excellency . . . But what?

JUAN

I didn't ask your name.

TISBEA
Me? Oh, I ent nobody, sir. Tisbea. A poor fishergirl.

JUAN
Tisbea, that's what I thought. The sea surge deafens me, my sweet, as it did surf-surfeited Odysseus, but I shall never forgive myself, I'll eat scorpions, that upon waking to the wonder of salvation I asked where I was, not your sweet name . . .

TISBEA
Tisbea, sir. And yours?

JUAN
Nobody. A shipwrecked prince. A poet.

TISBEA
A poet?

JUAN
What poet would triangulate his location instead of his feeling? No, I'm a boor, shipwrecked in need of faith . . . You are angelic, a fishergirl who knows her classics, with a limited library but a big heart, and I, I asked that shameless question, "Where am I?" rather than what I ask, in all remorse, "Who are you, Tisbea? And what's to become of us?" This repetition of immortal truth, this shipwreck, with only us . . .

TISBEA
There's a third . . .

JUAN

Who? Oh, him! Think of him as my shadow, my salt-sweet virgin, you are a virgin . . . ?

TISBEA

Sir, yes . . . yes . . .

JUAN

Shield your face from him, if you're abashed, then! Come, get up, Catalinion! You've lain there enough! Laurel your obscene girth with weed and take off . . .

(CATALINION *exits*)

TISBEA

Your metaphors, they're pure Homer.

JUAN

Sweetness, I've metaphors I haven't used yet. Oh, Eve of this new Eden, make me a suit of fig leaves. The serpent stirs. Do you know the first metaphor of Eden, Tisbea, the serpent? Do you know the winking one-eyed snake? Oh, let us pray the serpent (are you a Catholic? good) does not violate this sea-sprayed paradise; keep it down, down, like an eel, press, press this eel into its basket, sweet-salt fishergirl. We must be firm with it; here, put one hand firmly here, around its neck. That's right. Do you feel the monster, the devil, defying you?

TISBEA

Oh, sir, are you sure this is right?

THE JOKER OF SEVILLE   Act 1 / Scene 4

JUAN
> We must bring the old gospel to the New World! Hellfire and brimstone, white hoods of the Inquisition, Eden and the New World, voyages, shipwrecks, the wrath of God! Firmer, firmer, be firm with him, for Homer is just books, but this is the church; and they shall take the serpent by the neck and cast him out . . .

TISBEA
> He is very defiant!

JUAN
> Shake him, speak to him, defy him; he must be firmly firmly chastised, child . . .
>   (*To his loins*)
> Beast! Beast!

TISBEA
> I'm chastising, I'm chastising . . .

JUAN
> Well, but never release him, and we'll go over to . . . to that Eden there, my salty Eve, and cast him out, angel with the flaming sword. Keep the eel in the basket where it belongs, and lead us on, lead us on, there, in that grove . . . What kind of grove is that?

TISBEA
> Sir, oh, eucalyptus!

JUAN
> Pray with me.
> Come, come, come

Act 1 / Scene 4   THE JOKER OF SEVILLE

into that grove,
into that salt-sprayed eucalyptical Eden,
and we'll mix a couple of metaphors, Tabisha . . .

TISBEA
Tisbea, sir.

JUAN
      Come! Keep hold, keep hold!

(JUAN *and* TISBEA *exit. Music.* CATALINION *returns. A chorus of* FISHERGIRLS *enters, carrying baskets*)

FISHERGIRLS
Tisbea? Tisbea?

(CATALINION *approaches them. They draw back. A dance begins*)

CATALINION
Tisbea?
  (Sings)
Tisbea went and bathe,
a swordfish take she maid.
Tisbea, oh, oh!
Fire in the water!

(*In a frenzied, revivalist dance, the chorus of* FISHERGIRLS *lament* TISBEA's *seduction*

FIRST FISHERGIRL
Hold on to the rod,
Sister Tisbea!
Hold on to the roh-oh-od!

Though it turn like the staff of Aaron
to a miraculous serpent,
mind it jump out your hand!

SECOND FISHERGIRL
    (*Spoken*)
    Oh, what'll the priest say?
    What'll the priest say?

(*The dance becomes a brimstone-and-hellfire meeting. A* PRIEST *enters, preaching*)

THIRD FISHERGIRL
    (*Spoken*)
    What a way for a poor girl to get baptized!

FISHERGIRLS
    (*Sing*)
Tisbea went and bathe,
a swordfish take she maid.
Tisbea, oh! Oh, oh!
Fire in the water!

CATALINION
That rod is the rod
of correction,
but it point to the Promised Land;
it point to the Promised Land, girl,
but mind it jump out your hand!

FISHERGIRLS
Tisbea went and bathe,
a swordfish take she maid.

Act 1 / Scene 4 THE JOKER OF SEVILLE

Tisbea, oh, oh!
Fire in the water!

(*The dance ends. Voices off*)

ANFRISO'S VOICE
Tisbea! Why doesn't she answer?

FIRST FISHERGIRL
(*To* CATALINION)
That's Anfriso, he's so jealous,
if he finds out, he may kill her.
(*To the others*)
Run!
(*To* CATALINION)
Please, don't tell him you've seen us!

(FISHERGIRLS *and* PRIEST *exit.* ANFRISO *and* CORYDON, *two fishermen, with nets and fishing spears, enter*)

CORYDON
Anfriso! Look! A runaway slave!
Hold him! He survived that wreck.
You know how much money they'd give
to get a nigger like this back?

(*They charge* CATALINION, *who overpowers and sits on them*)

CATALINION
Now, what's this madness all about?

ANFRISO
Nothing. We thought you were a slave.

THE JOKER OF SEVILLE   Act 1 / Scene 4

CATALINION
>   I gathered that from your first shout.
>   But you should ask: "Are you a slave?"
>   like Christians; then colonize me.

ANFRISO
>   I'd like to be a Christian, but
>   I can't afford it—poverty.

(CATALINION *lifts and hurls them to the ground again*)

CATALINION
>   Buckle on faith, sharpen honor,
>   protect virgins while you butcher
>   black infidels, and there you are:
>   a Christian knight!

(*He steps away from them*)

ANFRISO
>   Aren't you a slave?

CATALINION
>   I was a Moor. Before this death,
>   it was conversion or the grave;
>   I was seized by your Christian faith.

CORYDON
>   How?

CATALINION
>   How, sir? In this position!
>   (*He seizes* ANFRISO *by the neck*)
>   This is how I was converted:

After a battle, as the sun
went down, I walked among the dead;
a righteous war, so every one
of its righteous warriors was dead,
and for that Heaven where they slept,
both sides had fought, both sides had prayed.
As I crouched by an elegant
cadaver, wondering to which Heaven
his soul had gone, because I'd sent
it there with all those righteous men,
my master crept up with his knife
and christianized me with the threat
that I should serve him all his life.
I'm paying off that little debt.

ANFRISO

So, where's your master? Did he drown?

CATALINION

In the bush. Doing something private.

(ANFRISO and CORYDON laugh)

CATALINION

It's private, but he's not alone.
He's found the New World; with his creed
he's now spreading her gospel wide
that all your women may be freed.

(ANFRISO and CORYDON move toward the bushes. CATALINION restrains them)

CATALINION
>I've sworn that while he's at his work,
>I'd guard him. So, let's search the wreck.

(CATALINION, CORYDON, ANFRISO *exit*)

SCENE 5

Dusk. The beach. Enter JUAN *and* TISBEA, *naked.*

JUAN
>Come, Tisbea, lift your head, be brave;
>the old world's dying and its grief
>is folded by the folding wave;
>walk naked in our new belief.
>I've spent a green life looking for
>one simple, unremorseful Eve.

TISBEA
>And, sir, all that you're looking for
>I hope I'll give like a good wife.

JUAN
>A wife? Well, back to the fig leaves!
>A wife! You calculating bitch,
>you're as heartless as the average
>virgin back there! What privilege
>comes from being Señor Tisbea?
>I must give up my life's belief

Act 1 / Scene 5 THE JOKER OF SEVILLE

>   for one more marriage? You appear
>   so weak you couldn't lift a leaf,
>   but what a weapon marriage is
>   to lambaste your ravaged honor!
>   God, you beasts must love your cages!
>   Marry a man, Tisbea; I am a
>   force, a principle, the rest
>   are husbands, fathers, sons; I'm none
>   of these. At that she shields her breast
>   in shame. Well, we're right back where
>   it all began. Where're you going?

TISBEA

>   To drown myself! What do you care?

(*She runs off*)

JUAN

>   But dress first, Eve! Put something on!
>   They don't like nakedness up there!
>   I'm going back on the next ship.
>   Old World, New World. They're all one.
>   Dammit! I hate a wasted trip.
>   Catalinion! Catalinion!

(*Exit*)

SCENE 6

The Spanish court: DON DIEGO, DON PEDRO, *the* KING OF CASTILE, DON GONZALO.

KING OF CASTILE
>A joke? My dear Don Diego,
>this joke festered. Naples will not
>forget what happened months ago:
>your son's hilarious exploit!
>The former union I arranged
>between Donna Ana and your son
>is therefore like this pact estranged.
>She'll marry someone else. That's done.
>Let it be Duke Octavio.
>We'll find him and we will restore
>his honor. I gave my promise
>to her and to Don Gonzalo.

DON PEDRO
>Sir, if I may say one word.

KING OF CASTILE
>No! No more exploits or fables.
>My dear ambassador, it's absurd
>to have the foreign policies
>of two great powers, Spain and Naples,
>balancing on your nephew's phallus!
>To rule both countries from a bed!
>He makes a brothel of a palace,

Act 1 / Scene 6   THE JOKER OF SEVILLE

and Christ knows what he's done abroad.
Who corrupts us corrupts Seville.
Speak, Don Diego! He's your son.

DON DIEGO

What can I say except . . . I've gone
past wondering at my son's ways, sir?
I preach to him of damnation,
but, sir, I am a widower . . .

KING OF CASTILE

He was a good boy, I know, I know.
Whoever was the devil's father
says the same goddamned thing.

DON DIEGO

A married, regenerate Juan
will settle into gentleness.
We've all had our wild days, we're men,
but marriage chastens all of us.

KING OF CASTILE

I don't want him dead, Don Diego,
just dutiful, provident. Till then,
the word is exile to Lebrija. Go!
Tell Naples in your own presence
I pronounced it. There's other business.
We've wasted too much breath on this.
That boy would ruin paradise.

(*Exit the* KING OF CASTILE, DON DIEGO, DON GONZALO. *Music*)

DON PEDRO
>Jesu Maria, what a mess!
>   (Sings)
>*The King of Castile has no sense of humor,*
>*the King of Naples cannot take a joke,*
>*and since I stand between each grim beheader,*
>*my head may lose its work!*
>*If I make one false move, repeat some rumor*
>*the King of Naples may have said a-*
>*bout the King of Castile, and that rumor spread, a*
>*war could accidentally break out.*
>*But everybody makes mistakes, friends,*
>*only Our Lord was flawless.*
>*That nature's a series of accidents*
>*is scientifically certain, well, more or less.*
>
>*Look, King! Did you know when you would be born?*
>*Poor purple infant, did you feel insulted?*
>*Or did you tell your parents, screaming on*
>*your royal entrance, "Why wasn't I consulted?"*
>*Or maybe the whole thing was a surpriser*
>*to your poor papa, when your ma, the Queen,*
>*broke the big news, and he died, none the wiser*
>*about the little accident you'd been!*
>
>*I wish I had your royal guts to tell you,*
>*frankly, or accidentally, to your face,*
>*that as a king you've better market value*
>*selling nuts at bullfights, you basket case!*
>*I've done all that I did to help my nephew, Juan.*
>*What have you damned kings done for poor Castile*
>*but sit there, turning purple on a throne,*
>*looking imperial? Big fucking deal!*

Act 1 / Scene 7 　　　　　　　　　　THE JOKER OF SEVILLE

If God wants life to go a certain route,
He causes accidents, and that's His sign.
Make one more mistake and you'll get a note
that I have accidentally resigned!

VOICES
(*Off*)
¡Olé!

(*Exit* DON PEDRO)

SCENE 7

Seville, dusk. A square. Bells tolling. Cheers from a bull ring. JUAN *and* CATALINION *enter.*

JUAN
　　Hypocrisy and gold: Seville!
　　She stinks of pride. Nothing changes
　　her pious smile, neither the smell
　　of corpses nor of oranges.
　　Christ! How she hardens my anger!
　　Her witch-hunting Inquisitors,
　　and her divine architecture
　　that was built by barbarous Moors.
　　It's Sunday. Lovers stroll in pairs
　　for the paseo, beautiful!
　　Meanwhile, the dying sun, with spears
　　irradiating from its skull,

vomits in sand, and the plaza
cornets sob for the broken bull.
>   (*Cheering from the bull ring.* RAFAEL *and his troupe, the* JACK,
>   *the* ACE OF DEATH, *and the* QUEEN OF HEARTS *enter and arrange
>   their theater: a cloth, a few properties*)

God, I hate actors! They refuse
to accept the reality
they live in! I pronounce these
solemn self-deceivers guilty
of doubling the dream that is life.
Watch this!
>   (*He crosses over to* RAFAEL)

        Sir, that catamite there
tucks his soft candle through his thighs
and simpers like an Infanta!

(RAFAEL *presents* JACK, *who is dressed as a girl*)

RAFAEL

No, no sir! All these gifts are hers;
she is my adopted daughter.
You could fondle the goods yourself,
except that they're not for sale. Her
beauty is all my worldly wealth.

JUAN

What does she play?

RAFAEL

        Sir, she portrays
Betrayed Love.

(CATALINION *comes over*)

Act 1 / Scene 7   THE JOKER OF SEVILLE

JUAN
             Don't tell me.
    (TO JACK)
                         You kill
yourself. A cliff. A watery grave.

RAFAEL
   Our art is life, sir, so it's still
   the only ending that we have.
   Anyway, we're just beginning.
   It's funny, too.

JUAN
             Ask her to sing.

RAFAEL
   Sing what, sir?

JUAN
                Come, ask the boy to sing—
   all of your women are boys—
   you ask your beauty to sing,
   and even with an unbroken voice
   I'll know.

RAFAEL
             Something melancholy?

JUAN
   Let her sing anything you choose,
   but nothing with carnality
   in it. I'm getting tired of that.

THE JOKER OF SEVILLE

Act 1 / Scene 7

Something that you feel would suit
that soiled face and unbroken heart.

RAFAEL
She knows one about a sea bird
that never finds a resting place.
"The Sea Bird," Niña.
   (JACK *whispers in* RAFAEL's *ear*)
                    Sir, she said
there is an instrument she plays
which ends the song. Well, get it then.

(JACK *exits*)

RAFAEL
You're a rich man, with possessions,
a servant, and all: we've met men
who believe that their positions
entitle them to slaves, and when
they point a finger, that's the end.
She's long in there.

(ACE OF DEATH *exits*)

JUAN
                    I'm different.
I work quite hard for what I get.

(ACE OF DEATH *returns*)

ACE OF DEATH
Rafael, I looked. The boy has gone.

Act 1 / Scene 7   THE JOKER OF SEVILLE

RAFAEL
> Gone?

JUAN
> The boy you said?

RAFAEL
> Gone! Gone where?
> I hope that I don't find him dead
> somewhere. And I hope you know why.
> Come on, we'll look for him. Come on.
> Niño! Niño! You want a song—
> listen to this one, then.
> (Sings)
> *In Sevilla, they give you the honor*
> *of calling you Don Juan, the Joker,*
> *and I call you too, El Burlador.*
> *But for me, now, that means the butcher.*
> *One day you will butcher no more,*
> *one day you will butcher no more.*

(RAFAEL, *the* ACE OF DEATH, *and the* QUEEN OF HEARTS *exit. Screams of laughter. Enter the* MARQUIS DE MOTA, MUSICIANS, *and two* WHORES)

DE MOTA
> Juan? Juan!

JUAN
> De Mota! Months! No, years!

(*They embrace*)

DE MOTA
> Didn't know you. You look so burned!

JUAN
>   How's my old whoremongering marquis?

DE MOTA
>   On his last visit to the Street
>   of Joy.

JUAN
>   Well, you've said that before.

DE MOTA
>   Ah yes, but remorse is still sweet.
>   It strengthens faith. And now, no more.
>   (*Sings*)
>   *Whatever happened . . .*

JUAN
>   You remember that? Our song to the Street
>   of Joy!

(*Music.* JUAN, DE MOTA, *and* WHORES *dance,* DE MOTA *swirling a red cape*)

JUAN and DE MOTA
>   (*Sing*)
>   *Whatever happened to Big-Foot Bertha?*
>   *What has become of Jane?*
>   *Where's Helen, who didn't like men to hurt her*
>   *in the same place twice again?*
>   *Where are the hags we found so pretty*
>   *in every port of Spain?*
>   *But more than all that, where is Lucy,*
>   *who took us both to bed?*

Act 1 / Scene 7   THE JOKER OF SEVILLE

Friends, that was in another country,
and besides, the wench is dead.

WHORES

Better forget about Big-Foot Bertha,
she don't work this beat again.
Helen and Jane got mixed up in a murder,
and besides, they were getting plain.
Life flies so fast, and youth is over,
and Lucy is on the wane.
So take what you see, and thank life, honey,
cause life begins in bed.
Life is a joke, but it ain't so funny
when that dingaling goes dead!

(WHORES and MUSICIANS exit)

DE MOTA

Shame! Sir! You see a reformed rake,
a man transformed by a vision.

JUAN

Transformed? Who? You? No, I can't take
this dry. Some wine, Catalinion.

(CATALINION exits)

JUAN

I'm hardly temperate, but I missed
the seasons, their mortal knowledge,
larks melting near the sun, the mist
of autumn, those hints of old age
that say there's so much left undone.

DE MOTA
>   Like what?

JUAN
>   Every virgin's honor.

DE MOTA
>   You must love or have loved someone.

JUAN
>   Almost. Once.

DE MOTA
>   Who? Do I know her?

(CATALINION *brings wine*)

JUAN
>   Her name's L'Alma. That business
>   ended quite well; we're friends, of course—
>   body goes one way, soul goes this;
>   it's been an amicable divorce.

DE MOTA
>   Juan, my friend. I've found a woman
>   I'd die for. She's sent this letter
>   to me. Listen . . .

(DE MOTA *shows a letter*)

JUAN
>   You, a husband!
>   I thought things were getting better.
>   Still, if it starts: "My dearest love,"

Act 1 / Scene 7   THE JOKER OF SEVILLE

and then its tone switches abruptly
to "Sweetheart, what is your next move,
or aren't you planning to corrupt me?"
she can be saved.

DE MOTA

              No. As each petal
shapes, by its scent, the emblem: rose,
for me each individual
virtue around that name coheres,
when I say: "Ana." I can't tell,
but it's like knowing there's a soul.

JUAN

Soul? . . . Jesus! You're not feeling well!
"And so it came to pass that Saul . . ."

DE MOTA

Who?

JUAN

        Paul! When this incorruptible
shall put on corruption, and when
corruption, quick as possible,
whips off its trousers once again!
There's no fiercer woman hater,
except possibly Augustine,
than that converted fornicator
who suddenly saw the lightning.

DE MOTA

   (*Crosses himself*)
God . . .

JUAN
           God? The New World that I saw
wasn't Eden. Eden was dead,
or worse, it had been converted
to modesty. No Indian goes
naked there; they're all dressed to kill
while the incense-wreathed volcanoes
hallow genocide. Eden was hell.
Men, earth, disemboweled for gold
to crust the Holy Spanish Cross.
Ah, knight, you're watching an age's
death. Chivalry, that flower you pressed
like a schoolgirl in the pages
of an old book, is drying fast;
those homilies from her Book of Hours
engraved by succubus-ridden
monks, dragons, Castles Perilous,
and the Just City, always hidden
round the next crag, are just as fake
as that Leviathan that was curled
round the horizon; the great snake:
belt for the belly of this world
that is all appetite! They're gone!
Gone, knight! Never to return!
The mystic Rose, the Quest, the Dragon
were used to tame and scare us! Tricks!
It has taken me years to learn
that dragon emblem is our sex,
that quest the siege of maidenhood,
that all our chivalry was the vexed
desire of flesh-starved lunatics
like coward fetuses who prayed

Act 1 / Scene 7   THE JOKER OF SEVILLE

in caves, afraid to go outside.
De Mota, pal, we've been betrayed!

DE MOTA

Juan, Juan, this is too wicked!

JUAN

All right, read what she's written you.
She loves you. And a rose is red.

DE MOTA

Her father's Don Gonzalo.
She was for a long time in Lisbon.
Please help me. Do not jeer. Listen.
(*Reads*)
"Beloved,
The King and my father want me to marry someone I cannot love; my husband's name and my father's new appointment will be announced together. On that day I may kill myself, since I will not be denied you. Tonight, come to my gate at eleven; wear your crimson-colored cape, so my maids will know. With my love, and my life, your Ana."

That's why I've brought this hood
and cape. After one last carouse,
my farewell to bachelorhood.
I'll wear it to Gonzalo's house.

(*A madman in rags,* ANFRISO *with horns made of knives, runs toward* JUAN)

ANFRISO

Toro! Toro!

(CATALINION *seizes him*)

62

THE JOKER OF SEVILLE Act 1 / Scene 7

ANFRISO
>A man needn't drink to go mad, toreros!
>World do that for you.
>Grief don't give a shit whether you teetotal
>or gutter rat, things pull you down.
>¡Olé! Love will do it. Horns will do it.

CATALINION
>Out! Get out!

(CATALINION *hurls him away*)

JUAN
>He's out to kill, the bloody fool!
>He's mixed me up with someone else.
>He says I tricked him, that bundle
>of dead rags! Who'd horn that carcass?

DE MOTA
>That's fame, torero! Take this cloak,
>and if he charges, use this sword
>to deal that mad bull its death stroke.

JUAN
>Use this as yours? I have your word?

(DE MOTA *gives* JUAN *his cloak. Thunder*)

DE MOTA
>Yes. It's suddenly cold! The sky's
>one slab of marble-colored cloud
>rumbles its tomb shut over us.
>You see that frowning thunderhead

Act 1 / Scene 7 THE JOKER OF SEVILLE

of marble? That's Don Gonzalo's
disapproval! Look there, lightning!
It flashed from the cathedral's yellow
face! There's cold sweat on the night's skin.

JUAN

It's our normal Spanish weather.
If you're that cold, take back your cape.

DE MOTA

No. Thinking of this endeavor
shook me. But I've a vow to keep.
Bring the cape to Gonzalo's house
before eleven. I'll meet you there.
You've a visitor. Your father.
He thinks I'm bad company, I'll go.

(*Exits*)

JUAN

                        And off he goes,
to sweat his terror out on whores!
   (DON DIEGO *enters*)
Sir. How did you know I was here?

DON DIEGO

By looking everywhere for you.
Hello, Catalinion.

CATALINION

            Señor.

DON DIEGO
> Your bold look from a hundred paces
> shatters your father's heart. Oh, Juan,
> you cannot know what his disgrace is.
> In you he sees his cracked reflection.
> But I didn't track you down to preach,
> I bore you enough. I've endured
> that dutiful smile, speech after speech,
> so I'll not speak as a father should.
> Your uncle, the ambassador,
> once the King asked him, had to tell
> how, disguised as Octavio,
> you tricked his Lady Isabel,
> thus violating that concord
> which married Naples to Seville;
> I bring his judgment like a sword
> to my own flesh.

JUAN
> What's it? . . .

DON DIEGO
> Exile.
> Exile or death.

JUAN
> Hilarious!
> I've just returned, and off I go!

DON DIEGO
> Everything's drained out between us,
> Juan. God knows why it should be so.

Act 1 / Scene 7   THE JOKER OF SEVILLE

    Drained, down to these dregs of duty;
    but when we meet, my cup is filled
    again with gall for the beauty
    of my fading, seraphic child.
    Was I too stern a widower,
    was my celibacy converted
    by that vow to your dead mother
    to a sick passion for the dead?

JUAN
    It's not your fault, sir . . .

DON DIEGO
                    Let her take
    that comfort, then, in her deaf grave,
    because her very stone would crack
    with sorrow at these jokes you make
    on women! Hurt one, you hurt her!

JUAN
    But when I please one, is she pleased?
        (DON DIEGO *slaps him*)
    So I'm my mother's murderer?
    But that same murder you think blest?
    Well, why defend my character
    against those who think they know it?
    What defense has any mirror
    against hate, except to show it
    as self-hate? I am their image,
    a question that has no answer.
    They smile, I smile. They rage, I rage.
    I feel nothing. I loved you, sir.

DON DIEGO
>Just as the devil loves his work!
>Bright rippled armor and dark mind,
>blazing with silver, but a lake
>that darkens slowly in the wind,
>like a cloud's shadow over wheat,
>your golden life will darken, Juan,
>and what they call your mischief, wit,
>corrupt your imagination.
>You're exiled to Lebrija. There
>I pray its parched desolation
>will turn your ecstasy to prayer,
>your joy to holy isolation.
>More than the King's, it's my own will.
>Let it be God's, as I'm His son.
>May love return by this division
>till that day when, across the wild
>and bitter gulf, father and son
>are reconciled, are reconciled.

(*Exits*)

JUAN
>Old statesman clouded with sorrow.
>That air of brisk efficiency
>he wears is an old cloak. I know
>the grief it hides. There's the penalty
>of loving one thing all our lives!
>>(*Pause*)
>On with this cape! And with it on,
>so this corruption shall put on
>incorruption and . . . It's nearly ten . . .

Act 1 / Scene 7   THE JOKER OF SEVILLE

CATALINION

>   First friend, then father. You can't be
>   going beyond them with some trick, sir?

JUAN

>   Call off my trick? You must be sick, sir!
>   Could I explain it to my prick, man?
>   Here comes Tenorio, your stickman!
>   Again we have to every virgin's grief
>   this tiger with a rose between its teeth.
>>   (Music. The MUSICIANS return. JUAN moves toward a balcony)
>>   (Sings)
>   *Oh, little red bird,*
>   *In your cage of ribs, tremble,*
>   *tremble and wait,*
>   *and he will come now.*
>   *The sky has no gate,*
>   *the open air is your temple,*
>   *every heart has the right*
>   *to its freedom,*
>   *every heart has the right to its freedom.*

(JUAN puts on DE MOTA's cloak, exits, then CATALINION)

SCENE 8

GONZALO's *house. Above. A bedroom.* ANA *at the balcony with her* DUENNA.

ANA

O God, it's hot! The stars are flying
like sparks across the smoky sky.
And somewhere, someone is dying,
someone is born. Will he come by?

DUENNA

I told him what you asked: to wear
his scarlet cape. And at eleven. He will.

ANA

You go to the gate below
the window.

DUENNA

         These stars shoot from Hell.
And a red cloak. That suits the devil.
Come on, come with me.

(DUENNA *and* ANA *exit. The street below: Darkness.* JUAN, *cloaked, enters, then* ANFRISO *as the madman, his knife drawn*)

ANFRISO

Don Juan Tenorio!

JUAN
> I've had enough!
Who are you?

ANFRISO
> Nobody. A man.

JUAN
> And all men die, so, man, come on!

(*They duel with cloak, sword, and dagger.* ANFRISO *dies.* JUAN *bends over the body*)

JUAN
> This madness they call Honor kills
> for the revenge of cuckoldry.
> Well, we're both mad! And mine now calls
> me from that iron balcony.
> One hour, friend, is all I have
> between your Hell and Ana's Heaven,
> between her bed sheets and your grave.

(ANA *emerges above*)

ANA
> Come over here. Hurry, hurry!
> Who're you talking to down there?

JUAN
> To no one. Nobody. That's his name.

THE JOKER OF SEVILLE

Act 1 / Scene 8

ANA

The gate is on the latch. But whisper.

JUAN

Whisper, fool, keep your voice the same.
(JUAN, *below, rehearses*—as DE MOTA)
I'm sorry I came earlier, sweet,
but I thought the sooner I got here
the better. There're patrols in the street
looking for a madman. Then the weather.
(*Himself*)
Christ, that's not it.
(As DE MOTA)
Ana, my sweet.

ANA

Yes?

JUAN

I came earlier,
because the sooner I got here . . .

(*Coughs*)

ANA

Hush, hush, what an unjust protest
when every jealous minute murders
time. Was that well-rehearsed?
But still in whispers. You're hoarse,
you hug the darkness. Come.

Act 1 / Scene 8   THE JOKER OF SEVILLE

JUAN

                Don't move!
The shame of passion in my face
deserves this mantling shadow; love,
before this act I should be bold,
but shame thickens and furs my voice;
besides, I have a sort of cold.

(*Coughs*)

ANA

I feel no shame. But this night air . . .
You're sweating!

JUAN

              It's the heart's fever.

ANA

For which, poor heart, there's the one cure.

(ANA *and* JUAN *exit. The cathedral bell strikes ten.* CATALINION *enters below*)

CATALINION

There's the hour. Ten dead strokes.
I was to meet him here and stall
the Marquis somehow. He likes his stakes
to be close, he gets a big thrill
out of that. I've got our horses
in the other street. That's all our life is—
mounting, dismounting. Hunts, chases.
I'm getting sick of it.

(*He stumbles on* ANFRISO)
>O Christ!

It's that blood-crazy matador.
Poor bull. Your face now. Anfriso!
Anfriso, you damned bloody fool,
did you come with us just to find your
honor? Oh, you look beautiful,
in your beautiful, sacrificial
revenge; now you're a knight,
a knight, aren't you? A cold formal
chivalrous lump of bloody meat.
(DE MOTA *enters the street. Waits*)
Congratulations! And there comes another
fool. With luck enough, he might
be your companion of honor.
I'll drag this hulk out of his sight.
Your attitude might put him off.

(CATALINION *pulls off* ANFRISO's *body, as* JUAN *appears*)

JUAN
You're early. Where's Catalinion?

(CATALINION *emerges*)

CATALINION
I'm here.

JUAN
>Your voice.

Keep your voice down. Where were you, man?

Act 1 / Scene 8 THE JOKER OF SEVILLE

CATALINION
> Waiting for you gentlemen, what else?

DE MOTA
> How was your cape work, beautiful?
> Where's your bull-headed madman? Gone?

(ANA *emerges above as* JUAN *gives* DE MOTA *the cape*)

JUAN
> I wounded him and chased him off,
> a tottering, blood-ribboned bull
> hugging the walls. I've had enough
> for one night. Here's your cloak.
> It's done enough veronicas.
> Come, Catalinion. We must run.

(CATALINION, JUAN *rapidly exit.* ANA *screams and runs off*)

DE MOTA
> Juan! What is it? That animal howl
> pebbled my racing blood to stone.
> My hair is freezing to my skull.
> It was the cry of birth. What woman . . .

(GONZALO *enters below, his sword drawn*)

GONZALO
> I couldn't sleep: watching the moths
> flinging themselves against the flare
> of torches. I thought, yes, they love
> like foolish women. I lay there
> magnifying every horror

THE JOKER OF SEVILLE　　　　　　　　　　Act 1 / Scene 8

    I heard, beyond its natural form:
    the cries of cranes threshing the air
    to silence. Then a woman's scream
    ripped the garden. I found Ana
    quivering from it. Let her see him!

(ANA *is brought out by the* DUENNA)

GONZALO
    She was to be Octavio's wife,
    not yours, but you'd do better now
    to savage her twice with that knife!
    Serpent who crept into my garden
    disguised as a god. Look now,
    you were a knight, sworn to honor
    women! Weep, serpent, for the new
    knowledge you have put upon her.

DE MOTA
    It was not I, sir. I'm not the one.
    Ana, tell him who it was.

ANA
    It was a man. Dressed in your crimson
    cloak. Your voice. I don't know.

DE MOTA
    I do.

GONZALO
        Who?

DE MOTA
> Juan Tenorio.

GONZALO
> > I should have known.
> Don Diego's son. He'll be caught soon.

DE MOTA
Where? He's running.

GONZALO
> > Let him run!
> He's running on my net; Seville
> will web him in labyrinthine
> alleys till, coil by tightening coil,
> that gladiator will be mine!
> He'll be caught.

ANA
> > Then kill him! Kill . . .

DE MOTA
Ana!

GONZALO
> He was to be her husband,
> then Naples wanted his exile.

DE MOTA
(*To* ANA)
You knew?

ANA
> No!

GONZALO
> It was my King's command.

DE MOTA

Your King's command. Another net?
You both knew!

ANA
> No! No! I did not!

(DE MOTA *struggles with his cape*)

DE MOTA

I'm in that net! O God, I'm torn
by spiders, a drunk fly, wrapped in
this leaf, but that's why flies were born.

GONZALO

Marquis!

ANA
> Love . . .

DE MOTA

Turn! If I looked in
those eyes, I'd only see my selves
webbed in their irises. O Christ!
let my trust return, or else . . .

(JUAN *emerges*, CATALINION *opposite him*)

JUAN
   Or else, give her up.

ANA
   Kill him!

GONZALO
            Don Juan . . .

DE MOTA
   Give her up, and what takes her place?

JUAN
   Another just as true as her.

DE MOTA
   For another like you to disgrace?

GONZALO
   Go inside, daughter.

JUAN
   No, let her see
   how chivalry dies one by one
   for her. Stay, lady.

GONZALO
                  You owe me
   your head, serpent.

JUAN

                In time, old man.
But each in turn. You're too old.
Restrain him, Catalinion!

(CATALINION *disarms* GONZALO)

JUAN

Marquis, let me make one thing plain,
and anyway, I have no sword.
Listen, what I took, de Mota—
I am a gentleman, on my word . . .

DE MOTA

God!

JUAN

. . . I took in your name, not mine.
It was to that name she gave all.

DE MOTA

Perhaps . . .

JUAN

                Send her to a brothel,
or convent, since Castilian
justice has simplified her choice
but not your self-righteous pity,
or my own little joke destroys
the truth, her love's virginity.

Act 1 / Scene 8

DE MOTA
　　A joke?

JUAN
　　　　Joke! Wasn't it you who said
　　the body is nothing, there's the soul?
　　Tell me, was her soul violated?
　　And tell me, don't you know it now
　　that she loves you, in soul and body?

DE MOTA
　　Juan, I have made my soul a vow
　　to kill you.

JUAN
　　　　I am ready.
　　Let the man go. Give him his sword.

DE MOTA
　　Defend yourself.

JUAN
　　　　No. You're absurd.
　　First, you think I have no defense
　　for what I've done. Then, I must fight
　　one of my dearest, truest friends?

DE MOTA
　　Juan, one of us will die tonight.

JUAN
　　Yes, but not for a woman's thighs.

ANA
    Kill him!

DE MOTA
            In God's name, then.

JUAN
                          No, say in life's.
    For if there's nothing in that cleft,
    that little Delphic mystery,
    but God, there's very little left
    to die for, between you and me.
    Two graves, one life, the second grave
    no more than an indifferent slit
    to take another stiff! Ah, save
    all that for-her-honor shit
    and go fight with some other friend.
    Or run me through if it
    suits you. I couldn't be more bored.

DE MOTA
    You are a fiend. A real fiend.
    There is the devil. I get cold
    looking at you. The honorable end
    would be to kill myself.

(DE MOTA *sinks to his knees*)

JUAN
                  Good! Be bold!
    Kill me, or yourself. Be Roman!
    Be like the noble knights of old

Act 1 / Scene 8   THE JOKER OF SEVILLE

and we'll sing, "He died for a woman."
   (DE MOTA *lifts up his sword*)
No, not the heart, the navel!
Lower, man, where God's finger
dented the clay; then I'll unravel
what mysteries are tangled there:
the divine augury of the gut—
that's very Roman, but we'll get
a Roman to read it. I cannot.

CATALINION
   Enough, master.

DE MOTA
               You leave me nothing.

JUAN
   You have my friendship. That's a lot
   for me, old friend. Give me that sword.
      (DE MOTA *weeps*. GONZALO *breaks from* CATALINION, *grabs* DE
      MOTA's *sword*)
   The fool's impossible! I will not
   fight you, sir. I must keep my word!
   Do not make me, I beg you, break it.

GONZALO
   No. You owe me that honor.

JUAN
   (*Screams*)
   I'll not fight you.

GONZALO
               If you're a man!

JUAN

    Do you see I beg him?
        (GONZALO *lunges and wounds* JUAN)
                Sir, you drew blood!

GONZALO

    For God's sake, fight me. One or
    the other, death or the redemption
    of my daughter's honor.

JUAN

    Sir, you're old,
    you rage with grief.
    Listen, if you die, you willed
    it, do you hear?

GONZALO

          I hear.
    I may be old, but tell your Moor
    that I've wasted, like him, thousands.

(*Music.* RAFAEL, *with a street crowd, and* STICKFIGHTERS *enter, forming a ring around the duel*)

RAFAEL

    (*Sings*)
Better watch yourself, old man,
nobody can beat Don Juan.
Better watch yourself, old man,
nobody can beat Don Juan!
    (*The chorus chants response*)
Send one man or ten thousand,
nobody can bend Don Juan.

Act 1 / Scene 8

*Send one man or ten thousand,
nobody can bend Don Juan!*

(GONZALO *falls*)

JUAN
Lives! You want mine! Nothing! A leaf
whirled in generations of leaves!

(ANA *rushes to her father's body*)

ANA
Papa!

GONZALO
Ana, daughter, I've gone
colder; but pray God it hardens
this heart to everlasting stone
cut with this last vow: "Vengeance!"

JUAN
"Vengeance is mine, saith the Lord."
But do you Christians listen? No.
For honor's sake you break God's word.
God must have nothing left to do.

(GONZALO *crosses himself, dies*)

DE MOTA
Ana, set his cold hands around
the sword, his cross. Mantle his eyes.
   (*To* JUAN)

THE JOKER OF SEVILLE   Act 1 / Scene 8

>His faith has found its proper wound,
>something your emptiness envies.

ANA
>Stare all you like. You won't see tears.

JUAN
>No. And I may not find answers.
>But back there in those cypresses
>in the garden, you knew who I was.

(ANA—*silence*)

DE MOTA
>The joke is hers. You tricked your wife,
>not mine. Let that torment you now
>as fiercely as her father's vow.

JUAN
>You will not answer?

(ANA—*silence*)

CATALINION
>The horses! I can hear the guard.

JUAN
>There's your sword.
>When that sad statue comes to life,
>both answer. Till then, not a word.

(JUAN, *then* CATALINION *exit*)
(*Drums, chanting. Music, as* GONZALO's *body is borne off by* STICK-FIGHTERS)

Act 1 / Scene 8

RAFAEL

(*Sings*)
O Lord, let resurrection come
from this stickfight!

CHORUS

O Lord, let resurrection come
from this stickfight!

RAFAEL

We cannot believe that death is champion—

CHORUS

In this stickfight!

RAFAEL

No, I will not believe that death is champion—

CHORUS

In this stickfight!

RAFAEL

O Lord, let resurrection come
from this stickfight!

CHORUS

O Lord, let resurrection come
from this stickfight!

(*All exit. The empty ring*)

Act Two

Without a painted paradise at the end of it . . .
EZRA POUND, *Pisan Cantos*

SCENE 1

Music. A wedding party. BATRICIO, *the groom;* AMINTA, *the bride.* RAFAEL *and musicians.*

WEDDING GUESTS
We have come from near,
we have come from far,
to see Batricio
marry Aminta.
        (AMINTA *and* BATRICIO *sit at the wedding table*)
And as is our custom
at all weddings,
I call on the bridegroom
to sing something,
for now is the last chance
he'll have to boast.

Act 2 / Scene 1   THE JOKER OF SEVILLE

*Then we'll sing and dance
to the marriage toast.*

(BATRICIO *rises*)

BATRICIO
*Friends, I'm no poet
as you will see,
but I'm proud that Aminta
has chosen me;
a queen so noble
deserves a prince,
but princes have trouble
and have no friends,
so to choose a peasant
was the right thing,
for the lady present
made me a king.*

(Applause. CATALINION *enters. Silence*)

CATALINION
We're tired travelers on the road
to Lebrija, when we saw this fete.

(JUAN *enters and congratulates* AMINTA)

RAFAEL
   (Sings)
*Mister, nobody is allowed
to talk here. You must celebrate,
and you must sing in rhyme, besides,
to toast Batricio and his bride.*

CHORUS
Improvise, you must improvise!

(*Applause: music. They form a ring*)

CATALINION
That prince who cannot turn his eyes
from your good wife, know who he is?

(*Silence*)

BATRICIO
You asking me, how I must know?

JUAN
I am Don Juan Tenorio!

BATRICIO
Because of that I must turn beast?

JUAN
We'd like to join your wedding feast.
    (*Applause*)
We hope it is all right with you.

BATRICIO
All right with me? Is that you hope?

(*Music*)

BATRICIO
    (*Sings*)
Man, invite the Queen,
man, invite the Pope,

invite the Duke of Edinborrow, I hope.
If the Queen can't come, then Lord have mercy,
invite the first feller you meet named Percy.
Take no heed of tomorrow,
don't mind the William,
I go beg or borrow
enough liquor to kill them.
This ent no damned country-bookie scene,
is me Batricio who marrying.
Invite the Governor, ring the Archbishop,
ring for more grog from the Chinese shop.
Invite the ugly, the short, and the handsome,
I ent care if it cost me a king's bloody ransom!
When it come to pay,
to hell with tomorrow.
Today is today,
I could beg or borrow.
   (All applaud. BATRICIO embraces RAFAEL)
A don from high cocoa-country
round San Rafael, this viejo knows
the grand court dances of Castile
before you slaves made calypsos
of everything. Don Rafael,
we have a prince here at this fete!

JUAN

>By right a prince should have the seat
>next to this bride.

BATRICIO

>   Then do it right.
>By ceremony. But there's one sweet
>place that you cannot take tonight.

THE JOKER OF SEVILLE   Act 2 / Scene 1

JUAN
   Where's that?

BATRICIO
              Where's that? Aminta, speak.

AMINTA
   A bed.

BATRICIO
           Aha!

AMINTA
              His bed and mine.

(BATRICIO, *laughing, withdraws*)

JUAN
   Yes, I can hear the bride-boards squeak
   like mice from that elephantine
   majesty, as the bedposts break.
   Where is that servingman of mine?
      (JUAN *claps.* CATALINION *approaches*)
   Look at them! Simple, country folk,
   et cetera, et cetera,
   but give them a chance, and they'll juck
   your eyes out, just like the bourgeois.
   This is no different from the court.
   Look at Batricio, drunk as hell,
   but one eye counting every draught.
   They have a king and queen as well.
   These slaves assert their heritage,
   but they despise their origins,

91

Act 2 / Scene 1   THE JOKER OF SEVILLE

so they dress up in the image
of courtiers, and bow to a prince,
playing at dukes and duchesses.
A sad joke, but a sadder lust
to curse their masters while they dress
like those who grind them in the dust.
My freedom isn't for the weak.

CATALINION
    So?

JUAN
    Draw the groom aside, that's all—
with some preliminary capework.

CATALINION
    Another day, another bull.
        (CATALINION *crosses to the wedding guests.* JUAN *returns to his seat near* AMINTA)
I'm giving the groom a present,
what does he like best of all?

WEDDING GUEST
    Best of all? Wine, women, cards.
In spite of them, he's a decent
feller.

CATALINION
    A gentleman peasant!
He has wine and wife. So, cards!
    (*Shouts*)
Batricio!

THE JOKER OF SEVILLE   Act 2 / Scene 1

BATRICIO
    Speak to me, I'm not a beast,
    even if tonight I'll be one.

CATALINION
    Cards! A chance, perhaps your best
    to pay all this.

BATRICIO
                Well, one quick round!

CATALINION
    Careful, Batricio, listen:
    Mankind isn't a house of cards
    structured that to remove one man
    collapses it. Look here! It's a game played
    for fun between a bored God and
    a bored devil. He's the Joker,
        (*Draws a joker*)
    that man who's kissing your wife's hand
    so chivalrously over there.
        (*Draws the ace*)
    Maybe God changes favorites.
    Listen, once it was the Moors,
    but we kept letting Him down. It's
    your turn in this game.

(*He tears the joker card*)

BATRICIO
                You're black,
    but I'll tell you, I'm worried
    about what's happening at my back.

Act 2 / Scene 1   THE JOKER OF SEVILLE

(*The card players freeze*)

JUAN
You have rude eyes.

AMINTA
              Rude?

JUAN
                     They're not quite
a bride's. They're a little restless . . .
Well, maybe they're just wet and bright
with expectation. Your nostrils . . .

AMINTA
Nostrils. Rude, too?

JUAN
            Oh, yes, they flare . . .

AMINTA
In anger, maybe . . .

JUAN
            No, at smells.

AMINTA
Smells?

JUAN
      The one which excites the mare.

THE JOKER OF SEVILLE

Act 2 / Scene 1

AMINTA
Now I'm a horse. The comparison
is odious for a prince. You must
pay praises to the stallion
who'll be my husband.

JUAN
                    And your breasts.

AMINTA
A cow's? Are you sure you're a prince?

JUAN
Yes.

AMINTA
Who thinks those below him beasts?

JUAN
You aren't below me, but that chance
will come tonight. And not a beast.
Rather a sacrificial lamb.

AMINTA
You think so? Did you hear me bleat?

JUAN
A sacrificial lamb, one laid
not on an altar but a bed,
revolving, slowly, on a sword.
You blush easily.

Act 2 / Scene 1 THE JOKER OF SEVILLE

AMINTA
>I don't, sir.

(WEDDING GUESTS *cross, greet, as they talk*)

JUAN
>I'll stake everything on this card.
>I'll bend toward that ear, whisper . . .

AMINTA
>Sir, I beg you, please, I'm married . . .

JUAN
>It's just a little joke, one word,
>and if that little ear goes red . . .

AMINTA
>I pay you?

JUAN
>>Your body, lady.

AMINTA
>Sir, my body has been given
>to one who is your host, already.

JUAN
>What else would make this bet even?
>The word I say has the one price:
>your priceless body. Come on,
>it'll touch that ear as lightly as
>a midge-hunting swallow's wing

touches the water, and is gone,
leaving ring after widening ring.

AMINTA

And all that in this word alone?
And that will bring me to your bed?

JUAN

No, but it may bring me to yours.
Just bend a little, there's no harm
in one word. Duchess, just one word.

(*He whispers to her*)

AMINTA

Sir . . .

JUAN

      You're blushing! Was it that bad,
duchess? You will be a duchess.
If you're devoted to a farm,
then make a farmyard of the court.
Aminta, with you on this arm,
I'd flash like a peacock, I'd strut
my prize so hard, young cockerels
would shake their wattles, fan their tails
to pluck you from me; the King's eye
will bulge like cross-bred carbuncles;
old hens will stagger from their roost,
blighted with envy! Don't laugh! It's less
funny than you think. The rest
of your life could be bitterness.

(*He rises, bends to her*)

Act 2 / Scene 1   THE JOKER OF SEVILLE

AMINTA

    You're joking, yes!

JUAN

                  In the sense that all
passionate postures are comical,
perhaps; but I'm dead serious!
Duchess Aminta.

AMINTA

              Me? Duchess?

(*Laughs. Music*)

JUAN

    Laugh. I must mingle with your guests.
But, love, remember what I've sworn:
that that white body, those white breasts,
whose whiteness would have drawn the swan
from staggering Leda, is my own,
not Jupiter's, not your husband's.
They've struck up the Manzanares.
Duchess, may I have this dance?

AMINTA

    Batricio?

BATRICIO

          Get those fiddles grating
like cicadas, make the bass bow
thump like bullfrogs till grog raining
down every guest dry gullet! Blow!

(JUAN *dances with* AMINTA)

THE JOKER OF SEVILLE

Act 2 / Scene 1

QUEEN OF HEARTS
(Sings)
O River Manzanares,
Run, run and ask my love
if her brown sapodillas ripe, in
that little orange grove;
and if she tell you yes, yes,
keep quiet, Manzanares,
I so hungry inside.
O Virgin, I so hungry!
Don't tell the Rio Cobre,
he'll run and tell the sea,
and the sea' mouth too wide.
Yes, yes, yes, Manzanares,
I know you can't run back
to tell me, you're a river,
but my mind is a river
and rivers have one track.
I want those sapodillas,
I want them, Manzanares,
I want that orange wine,
you hear me, Manzanares?
Say: I coming downriver,
for what she said was mine.

(The wedding party applauds. AMINTA runs to BATRICIO, who rises from his gambling)

BATRICIO
Come on! I've had enough of this!
I've lost, but my wife wins a kiss.
What's money when tonight's business
is coming? That red-faced, wine-pissed

Act 2 / Scene 1

sun has already gone to bed,
so should Batricio! Wait inside
on those white moonlit sheets, prepared
to greet Batricio as his bride.

(AMINTA *exits, and* WEDDING GUESTS *disperse.* JUAN *circles the wagon*)

CATALINION

Wake up, Batricio, and look!
That man there who is circling
your wagon is a golden hawk
charming your chicken.

BATRICIO

                      Playing peacock!
Know what's a peacock? A vulture
with money! If I had the luck
of being born rich, I'd have culture.

RAFAEL

A peacock? No! What I saw was
a wasp stuck in your wedding cake,
trembling with venom. But she's yours,
Batricio, and, for all our sake,
don't thrash round in that sea of lace
like a walrus: be firm, but kind.
Love her with mastery, but grace;
gentleness conquers womankind.

(RAFAEL, CATALINION *exit.* JUAN *moves toward* BATRICIO)

JUAN

Stride gently, like a gentleman,
toward her bed. Sir, I'm a prince . . .

BATRICIO

>Peasant or prince, a man's a man.
>It makes no fucking difference
>to me. I have a woman, white
>and quiet as a candle there,
>and I'm going to set her alight!
>Move, Prince! Your pride infects the air.

JUAN

>Excuse my mood. Sometimes, even
>the stars look sullen. Tonight they
>sulk, instead of shine in heaven,
>and I've caught their melancholy.
>You're drunk, can you still value friends?
>My soul has something to confess.

BATRICIO

>Better to spit it out. Look, Prince,
>those friends I lost when I was drunk
>can stay lost. They weren't really friends.
>I'm not the peasant that you think.

JUAN

>Yes, you're a peasant, but you see . . .

BATRICIO

>Not a peasant, by no means, not!
>Landowner! Man of property.
>Got fifteen drakes, what else I got? . . .

JUAN

>A bride who isn't really yours.

Act 2 / Scene 1 THE JOKER OF SEVILLE

BATRICIO
>Not mine? They call you the Joker
>for good reason. Read these papers:
>my license, here! Read! I bought her!
>She cost a fortune. I should laugh:
>"A bride who isn't really yours!"
>Joker, that one joke was enough.

(BATRICIO *draws out a knife*)

JUAN
>But what you've bought is slightly used.

BATRICIO
>Used? By whom? Shut your filthy mouth!

(JUAN *disarms, then grabs* BATRICIO)

JUAN
>Listen! Now drive this through your skull,
>you pig-eyed, pea-brained behemoth.
>You lily-kneed ox, you barrelful
>of tripe and garlic, you twice-pissed,
>dirt-clotted, voluntary bull,
>don't bellow at me, I'm your guest!
>You think I'd risk my life, you fool,
>if I didn't have to? I'm dismayed!
>I know you're a man of honor,
>I spoke from honor. But I've made
>a mistake. When dawn breaks on the
>cracked mud flats of that drying brain,
>you'll be the oldest joke, poor bull
>who'll be the laughingstock of Spain

for stumbling into the wrong stall
his wedding night. In spite of friends.
I tell the truth, and there, you see,
the stars turn in indifference.

BATRICIO

No. Tell me the truth. I'm ready.

(JUAN *gives* BATRICIO *the knife*)

JUAN

If my life redeems your honor,
take it. About a year ago
I passed here, I met Aminta,
I was a prince, and she . . . No, no!
Please! Rather than have us weeping
with shame and hatred through this night,
let's lock this secret in our keeping,
the three of us. That is the right
and good thing, than to discover . . .

BATRICIO

O God!

JUAN

    We didn't know what wrong
would breed from it. Who can ever?
  (Pause)
What is it?

BATRICIO

    I've bitten my tongue.
Well, I'm sober now. Tell me more
proof and I'll tear up these papers.

Act 2 / Scene 1   THE JOKER OF SEVILLE

JUAN

    Didn't you see how she greeted me,
    like an old friend? The smiles, whispers?

BATRICIO

    Yes, yes, I couldn't always see
    you, but my shoulders were like ears
    straining while I was playing rich
    there. I was shamed of jealousy,
    but I was right. Treacherous bitch
    that I paid so much money for!
    She cost me more than a good batch
    of hunting dogs.

JUAN

               The exchange is fair
    because you've lost nothing, you'll save
    the dogs' cost and your pride.
    You are a Christian. Try. Forgive.

BATRICIO

    Never!

(*He tears up the papers*)

JUAN

    Jealousy is human.
    And her shame, too, as a used bride.

BATRICIO

    I have no use for a used woman.
    I have my honor and my pride.

JUAN
> Yes, pride, which must be merciful
> as princes. Non-consummation
> tonight on both sides cancels all,
> saves her and your reputation.

BATRICIO
> Sir, I thank you. You're a true prince.

JUAN
> And you, noble Batricio. Cry
> if you must, a strong man cries once;
> then he endures all silently.
> That makes us noble, so goodbye.

BATRICIO
> Oh, please give Aminta this ring.
> Tell them goodbye for me, my guests.
> Listen, Rafael is still singing.
> I know my soul will never rest.

(BATRICIO *exits.* RAFAEL *and troupe return. Music*)

RAFAEL
> (Sings)
> *There is a sower in the sky*
> *who sows the seeds of stars;*
> *that sower's name is death, my lord,*
> *who sows that we shall die.*
> *And if I die before you, love,*
> *the harvest that I reap*
> *will be the memory of our love*
> *through everlasting sleep;*

Act 2 / Scene 1

*in everlasting sleep, my love,
in everlasting sleep.*

ACE OF DEATH and QUEEN OF HEARTS
*Everlasting sleep,
everlasting sleep.*

JUAN
Aminta?

AMINTA
Batricio. Come.

(*She opens the wagon's tent flaps.* JUAN *approaches*)

JUAN
Lift the bride lamp a little higher,
poor foolish virgin. The bridegroom
your heart honestly seeks is here.

AMINTA
You've drunk enough, come in and rest.
What are you out there mumbling?

JUAN
And as he enters the lamp's ring,
he sees its glow ripen your breast
to golden apples. He sees
it fleck with russet points that hair
which night has loosened to the stars.
I am not Batricio.

(JUAN *enters the wagon*)

THE JOKER OF SEVILLE   Act 2 / Scene 1

AMINTA
                    Murderer . . .

JUAN
   Let me in. Batricio's not dead.

AMINTA
   Where's he?

JUAN
                    Gone. You need a nobler
   body to consecrate that bed.

AMINTA
   He'll kill you. I beseech you, sir,
   respect my marriage. You must go.

JUAN
   I am here for its annulment.

AMINTA
   Good. Tell that to Batricio.

JUAN
   He knows. This is with his consent.
   He sends this ring for you to see.

(*He shows her the ring*)

AMINTA
   No man can be that arrogant!

Act 2 / Scene 1 **THE JOKER OF SEVILLE**

JUAN

> The essence of humility
> is this: to plead with another.

AMINTA

> Or humble them as you do me.
> Sir, I have taken a solemn oath
> of marriage.

JUAN

>   You will keep that vow
> to me in there; for that vow's truth
> is greater than you who have sworn it.
> Give me the lamp. Look, in those eyes
> the truth shines as I first found it
> when I first praised them. Not the lies
> of contracts, churches, marriages.
> Aminta, speak what they confess;
> that I should be your husband, not
> that boor Batricio. Those eyes . . .

AMINTA

> Show you my soul afraid of this
> sacrilege of my body's vow.

JUAN

> Yes, while my soul in wretchedness,
> manacled in the body's vise,
> still sings, inside its cage of iron,
> upon its bone rack, praises of
> your body's everlastingness.
> That is our misery: to love
> the very prison that we're in.
> And when love comes to free us, is

redemption by the body sin?
This ring delivers to your hand
my soul and body. Then wear it,
and what a wife gives her husband
give me, with body, soul, and heart
in all your body's nakedness;
and where your wedding lace has set
those fern-like patterns on your skin,
and where that small salt rivulet
is trickling between banks of fern
down to where deeper ferns divide:
Aminta, let your husband in.
I speak as bridegroom speaks to bride.

AMINTA

Then let my husband's will be done,
because God has blest me. I'm still
a bride, but more: a royal one.

(*She blows out the lamp, and* JUAN *moves toward her. Darkness.* JUAN *rises from the bed and watches* AMINTA *asleep*)

JUAN

I'm being ground down by my will.
These easy victories aren't fun
any more. This takes my exile
to its farthest point. I can't run
to some remorseful desert while
there's a role my life has chosen:
to play the Joker of Seville,
so, back to Seville I'll return.

(*Exit. Dawn. The* WEDDING GUESTS *rise from the field, leaving.* AMINTA *rises. Music*)

Act 2 / Scene 2   THE JOKER OF SEVILLE

AMINTA

(Sings)
*In the morning,
in the morning,
I was no longer married.
Tell that to the ground dove
in the field of brown corn.*

*In the sunrise,
in the sunrise,
I was no longer a virgin.
I gave him permission.
O white rose of morning,
O red rose of sunset,
tonight, tonight,
I will be sleeping alone.*

SCENE 2

Seville, a room in the palace. ANA, *alone, then* ISABELLA.

ANA

Desolate, desolate terraces
that I keep haunting for nothing;
where every archway utters his
figure, while my steps are echoing
absence. O Father, I have tried!
But no distraction's possible
for me! My eyes haze when I read.

When I'm embroidering, I feel
as if my stabbing needle's thread
sewed you forever in the earth.

(ISABELLA *enters*)

ISABELLA

You mind my being barefooted?
I've been wearing shoes from birth.

ANA

My name is Ana de Ulloa.
Sorry I stared.

ISABELLA

        I'm Isabel.
I go barefoot from habit, also
in honor of the Barefoot Nuns,
because I was one. How are you?

ANA

I was Gonzalo's daughter. Once.

ISABELLA

I came here at our King's command.
In pity for Don Diego;
his son, Juan, will be my husband.

ANA

And mine, the Duke Octavio,
when it's the Marquis that I love.
But we're women, what can we do?
We can't protest, we can't approve.

ISABELLA

We'll sink like cattle to our knees
and thank that manipulator
of our stock price: after all, he's
royally found us a buyer,
a bit reduced, but their concern
is for negotiable meat,
and so I'm given back to Juan,
honorably now, to be his mate.

ANA

That serpent flashed into a sword
and struck my father! Over his
cold body that snake who murdered
him swayed with cold, remorseless eyes.
Oh, sister, I know how our mother
Eve must have felt in that garden!
Naked with knowledge I stood there,
too wise to ask Adam's pardon
or my dead father's. I just stood
there, soiled and speechelss with its seed.

ISABELLA

I've know that silence, and its word
is wisdom.

ANA

       You are mad, they've said.

ISABELLA

Mad, oh, yes! I've known what it is.
I went in silence to my cell,
stripped of bodily desires,

prepared, as Sister Isabel,
to be lost among novices
as snow loses itself in snow,
with white, sacramental whispers.
Then came those nights my prayers would grow
into a monstrous wind that hissed
obscenities, whipping me round
and round, until in that tempest
I fell from a whirlwind. I'd rend
my sad sweating flesh with questions
till the questions turned ecstasies
and I stopped asking them. Then, once,
I, who'd been avoiding mirrors,
entered one cautiously, and stared
and stared, until a little smile
wiser than I had understood
eased my whole body, and I passed
into that after-storm-serene
light that makes the heaving tempest
more beautiful from its breakdown.
I sailed into a calm of love
deeper than man's. My heart was drawn
into the holiness of life.
Where once I couldn't lift my head
to dragons martyred on stained glass,
where, locked in paralyzing lead,
the saints were brightly jeweled flies
for God, the spider, I saw now
all endured, and all surrendered!
My agony had made life new
and endless as the unhindered
sky when it is a seamless blue.
O Ana, my sister, just as

translucent leaves at evening show
their veins to us, my body was
a house for that suffusing glow
that came from the sun of my self.
I thought it was desire, not knowing
till now that it was something else,
the love which surrenders loving
to become love. Its name is grace.
And I had owed this power to Juan.
The tears were streaming from my face—
tears, expressing no expression,
for the new freedom that was ours
as women. He taught us choice.
He, the great Joker of Seville,
whose mischief is simply a boy's,
has made us women, that is all.

ANA

All? If you'd seen your father's death,
his face, graying to stone, you'd hate
his murderer. With my last breath
I'll pray for justice, and for both
of you, until he pays that debt.

(AMINTA, *absurdly gowned, enters*)

ISABELLA

Now, who's this bright, breathless lady?

AMINTA

I'm the Duchess of Lebrija
to-be. I was sent here. Today

I'll meet the King, and then prepare
my guest list with his majesty.

ANA

Then, is your husband also here—
the Duke, I mean?

AMINTA

               Oh, momently!
(*Pause*)
Oh, it's no deep secret, madam.

ANA

I'm not married.

AMINTA

             Oh, you should be!
You'd be less nervous than I am,
Miss . . .

ANA

         Ana. Here's Isabella,
Duchess of Naples, whom her love
makes just as happy as you are.
This also is her nuptial eve.

AMINTA

Delighted to meet you, Duchess.
My God, isn't this place immense?
I feel so small. How is my dress?
More subtlety, and less expense,
was what my duke, Don Juan, advised.

Act 2 / Scene 2   THE JOKER OF SEVILLE

ANA
   Who?

(ISABELLA *laughs*)

AMINTA
           Juan. What's the big joke, madam?

ISABELLA
   Nothing, nothing.

AMINTA
                    I feel absurd.

ISABELLA
   It's not you.

ANA
           No, it's the wisdom
   that Sister Isabella learned
   from isolation. She'll share some
   of it with us, if we're patient.

ISABELLA
   Your husband's marrying me as well!

AMINTA
   Laugh! If I were differently dressed,
   you'd see a different spectacle!
   I'd have ripped this whole damned palace
   to shreds. But that's too comical.

ANA
   Smile, at the priceless comedy
   of my father's murder! Duchess,

116

I can see now that there's something
in your humor that matches his.

ISABELLA
Listen, Ana, don't you see
that what he's shown the lot of us
is that our lust for propriety
as wives is just as lecherous
as his? Our protestations
all marketable chastity?
Such tireless dedication's
almost holy! He set us free!

(DON PEDRO *enters as a steward*)

DON PEDRO
Duchess, the King awaits you all.

ISABELLA
Don Pedro? Have you been reduced
to opening doors?

DON PEDRO
               Yes. Pride will fall,
but folly falls farther. I'm used
to this. Actually, this sort of thing's
more my speed than signing treaties.
   (*He signals* ISABELLA *apart*)
Pssst!
      Will you tell me why the King's
summoned you both? You three? Who is
to be, at last, my nephew's bride?
And won't this marriage pardon Juan?
   (ISABELLA—*silence*)

All right, then, Duchess, go inside.
   (*He pounds his steward's rod. It breaks*)
O Christ, another damned rod gone!

(ISABELLA *and* ANA *exit.* AMINTA *waits. She signals to* DON PEDRO)

AMINTA
   You! Come!
      (DON PEDRO *crosses to her*)
            The King married? Sorry,
   but I'm not leaving here without
   at least a duke. I spent money
   to get here.

DON PEDRO
            A duke, eh? This court
   is one great fairyland of dukes,
   if they're the sort you're looking for.
   But a fresh, rational girl with looks
   like yours needs something more mature.
   You've an elemental nature,
   and the great thing about nature
   is how she heals herself, rather
   than brood and pine. It's laughter
   of a deeper sort.

AMINTA
            His Majesty's
   waiting, sir.

DON PEDRO
            There's just one thing more.

AMINTA
   What's that?

DON PEDRO
>   May I? You have rude eyes.
>   (AMINTA *laughs*)
> Someone has told you this before?

AMINTA
> Yes, but I'm starting to forget
> his name.

DON PEDRO
>   I love the way you laugh.

AMINTA
> Well, sir, a certain Joker taught
> me this same laughter that you love.

(AMINTA *and* DON PEDRO *exit, laughing, arm in arm*)

SCENE 3

Seville: a fountain near the cathedral, dusk. OCTAVIO *and* RIPIO *enter.*

OCTAVIO
> Today my Isabella's freed
> from her cold convent, but my cell
> is still my vow. Ripio, I've tried
> for one year to be merciful.
> For one whole year I fought those sins
> that make us mortal. It went well.

Act 2 / Scene 3   THE JOKER OF SEVILLE

> At Santa Cruz the Capuchins
> took me into their cool chapel,
> and there the gentle brethren laid
> my body out in oil, in leaves,
> to cure the unseen wounds that bled
> for love. My flesh was fresh as loaves.
> But, Juan Tenorio, what you've done
> is worse than any woman's loss.
> You've crucified me with a crown
> of thorns, that now, when I confess,
> the wafer clogs my gullet, wine
> is gall! Gall! Now you say the news
> is that he's taking sanctuary
> in the cathedral?

RIPIO

             Yes.

OCTAVIO

             How nice!
> How whorish of that church to be
> there when that heretic needs her now!
> On this, the anniversary
> of All Souls' Eve, of my year's vow,
> my King will pardon him at court?

RIPIO

> Yes. If he'll marry Isabel.

OCTAVIO

> Before that snake crawls near her skirt
> again, even for mercy, I'll
> lop its head off. No, God, not that!
> If he repents, I'll spare him; if

not . . . I'll lead him down to Hell
where he can lace the devil's wife
and add two horns to the devil.
All right. My joke begins. The sack—
in that sack there's the old robe, eh?

RIPIO
  Yes.

OCTAVIO
    Things go in cycles, Ripio. Shock
and readiness. Well, the circle
that's the New World brought him right back
to where it started, in Seville.
Come, you'll wait over there, the Moor's
your responsibility. Do well!
  (RIPIO *exits*)
O sea-green hills the crossing gull
called Santa Cruz: lemon orchards
sailed from her wing, and a chapel:
La Divina Pastora. Woods
and a heard river soothed me there.
  (*Music*)
  (*Sings*)
O Divina Pastora,
Holy Shepherdess,
I see that valley still
in times of stress,
seas of bright grass
where, like a pearl, my soul
sleeps in its shell of grace.
Ah Pastora Divina,
Holy Shepherdess.

*Let my heart find
that peace that leaves emotion
far behind.
Let my mind
lie in that sea-green valley with no motion
but the wind.*

*I am a driven gull,
seeking those seas
past restlessness,
where every rolling hill
is like a wave which stays
stilled by the hand of grace.
O Pastora Divina,
Holy Shepherdess.
O Divina Pastora,
Holy Shepherdess.*

(Exit)

SCENE 4

Seville. A fountain before the cathedral. JUAN and CATALINION enter, travel-stained.

CATALINION

This must be Hell, not just Seville.
It's fierce enough to char your soul.

THE JOKER OF SEVILLE   Act 2 / Scene 4

JUAN
> When we hide in the cathedral,
> you'll soon start bitching how it's cold.
> In that convent: nuns, novices!
> You think they sleep well these hot nights?

CATALINION
> I'm thirsty.

JUAN
>   God, to be a breeze
> inquiring into their habits!

CATALINION
> (*Laughs*)
> You're a married man. What a price
> you have to pay for having done
> in Don Gonzalo.

JUAN
>   Christ! Marriage!
> I marry Isabel or burn
> life out in barren Lebrija.
> Till then: sanctuary. In church.

CATALINION
> The bloody fountain's dry. Look here.

(JUAN *looks into the fountain*)

JUAN
> There's . . . water . . .

Act 2 / Scene 4 THE JOKER OF SEVILLE

CATALINION

      Water? There's a mulch
of rotting leaves. They're bad for thirst.

JUAN

I'm telling you I saw water!
This is dead summer's vengeance: dust
trickling from the stone lion's jaw,
and heat that topples the locust
back into the basin's furnace.
But I saw water and I saw
as if through glass a dead man's face.

CATALINION

The waves of heat brought that mirage.
In the desert, when you're tired,
you see monsters.

JUAN

     Circle the edge.
Look in the basin.

CATALINION

     There's a thick
toad hunched in the heart of the basin.

JUAN

It almost has the heraldic
immobility of a god. Begin.
 (*He kneels*)
O wound I envy, spring again

THE JOKER OF SEVILLE   Act 2 / Scene 4

    like this fountain, drench me in blood!
    Lead me through a fine mist of rain
    toward love. Love is the good pain.
    He blinks once. And I'm nothing.

(A bell tinkles. The ACE OF DEATH enters, dancing, followed by the QUEEN OF HEARTS and RAFAEL, pulling a little wagon with the statue of DON GONZALO. JUAN rises from the fountain)

RAFAEL
    (Sings)
Princes and peasants, kneel in fear and fart!
Here comes the harvest of the charnel cart.
Here comes the scyther with his tinkling bell.
Here's your old troupe of mummers with their art,
their painted Heaven and their painted Hell.

ACE OF DEATH
    (Sings)
Now here's the statue of a famous man,
General, Commander, Prince among men.
Isn't it lifelike in death, or was it
that in life he was death-like anyway?
Stern-visaged, moral, rigid, a mold
of what death had to cast him from someday?

(JUAN approaches, circling the statue and the dancing troupe)

RAFAEL
    O Prince, Commander, never more noble
    than in this image, stern, correct, immobile!
    Object of admiration, height of awe,
    your death was worth this statue we adore.

Act 2 / Scene 4   THE JOKER OF SEVILLE

ALL

> Amen, amen, amen, amen.

JUAN

> I remember you: the actor
> in a cheap farce, "El Burlador,"
> that stank like the rotting laughter
> it roused. Where's your boy-girl singer?

RAFAEL

> Ah, well, your honor, in this trade
> every man so catching his arse
> we soon resemble, I'm afraid.
> Boys have a way of getting lost.
>   (*Introduces his troupe*)
> This "jamette" always plays the Queen,
> this death's-head our Emperor,
> and so forth. And I make dead men
> on the side now, since from actor
> to statue is a mere matter
> of talent, and any piss-poor
> performance shows you when it's true.
> I carved this Knight of Calatrava
> to flog him to the convent, so's
> he can strike eternal terror
> in the hearts of poor novices
> who feel like straying from the path.
> You can either guess who he is
> solemnly or have a good laugh.

JUAN

> It's terrible.

RAFAEL
          He's for the church.
Perfect posture, no bloody voice,
or he'd be a miracle. He's much
more everlasting than dead boys.

JUAN
    (*To the statue*)
There's a farm girl in Lebrija
practicing to be a duchess.
People always want to be higher
than they are. Haven't you found this?

CATALINION
The eyes . . .

RAFAEL
              Kneel, read his inscription.
It's in Latin.

JUAN
            A dead tongue. Pompous
and perfect for a tongue of stone.
Vengeance!

CATALINION
        The eyes follow us.

RAFAEL
Recognize him?

JUAN
            Of course. This fool
kept practicing for his statue.

Act 2 / Scene 4   THE JOKER OF SEVILLE

So tell me, sir, how do you feel,
one plinth above your old stature
and weighing one stone heavier?
I got you there where you belong:
under the pigeon's quick opinion!
Honor! Look, Catalinion!
What was he famous for? It's gone.

CATALINION

When the sun has gone, the gnats rise.
It's always so with a great man
toward his twilight. When he dies,
gossip nibbles reputation.

JUAN

He grows in rigor, the stone goat!
Ay, goat-face! Did you comb your beard?
Have supper with me, then, tonight!
I guarantee you I'll be bored,
but I'll still listen. What? You can't.
Well, that's a pity, isn't it?
Never got to know each other
formally, did we? All you thought
of me was: your daughter's lover.
Goat, when a knight asks you to dine,
you should bleat back! What did he say?
Stone bread, stone cheese, and a stone wine?
Well, I can't promise, but we'll see.
By the way, for the time being,
I live in church. For sanctuary.
Good night, then. Hope to be seeing
you dead at midnight, and forgive

THE JOKER OF SEVILLE   Act 2 / Scene 4

    the pun. Tomorrow I'm marrying
    Isabella, if I'm alive.

(JUAN *and* CATALINION *exit.* OCTAVIO *emerges as a friar*)

OCTAVIO
    I'm certain you know who that was.

RAFAEL
    Don Juan Tenorio. A prince.
    I know both who and what he is
    from my bitter experience.
    You, I don't know. A priest, of course.

OCTAVIO
    Octavio. I want him killed.

RAFAEL
    Kill him yourself, though I have cause
    to make that Joker twice as cold.
    I'd a boy once: my little Jack,
    that mortal angel played women
    because he'd a voice like the lark
    rising. He'll never sing again.

OCTAVIO
    I knew your loss. We share one hate.
    Sir, with one last joke on that man,
    your greatest triumph lies ahead!

RAFAEL
    Triumph? In my exhausted span,
    I've lost all savor for success

Act 2 / Scene 4   THE JOKER OF SEVILLE

since the boy died; all elation
in applause, this grinding business
of fame. I'm just an old actor
who's been beating these boards for years,
playing the same old character,
more dried out than this fountain is.
I'll tell you, sir. You should a' come
years gone. I played a great king, once.

OCTAVIO

The king could get back his kingdom.

RAFAEL

Seville has better actors. Kings,
queens, jokers, knights. They're more alive.
I'm like this fellow here, sir, dead.
The theater has eaten my life.
I've no regrets, mark you. I've led
this company for fifteen years;
some of the best I've forfeited,
some reasonably turned traitors
for more cash: but the tears don't come
again; for mockery or applause.

OCTAVIO

Since you're dead, then, couldn't you play him?

RAFAEL

No lines? Yes.

OCTAVIO

            You'll wear what he does,
your face rigored marble, your eyes

    lashed white with dust, your grave voice
rotted with damp, your hand green ice.
Your vow, vengeance. Here's half the gold.

(*He pays* RAFAEL)

RAFAEL
    You tell me why I should do this.

OCTAVIO
    Because I dream.

RAFAEL
              Dreams can't do good
or harm. Come. Speak it out. Confess.
Wring it from your heart, word by word.
All that bitter silence does
is draw venom deeper inward.

OCTAVIO
    There is a garden. In its hush
a woman sprawls to greet the snake,
its adze-head nuzzling her bush.
My cold sweat turns to scales just like
the thing I should abhor. I change
into the serpent, too, sometimes,
and it's my body and not Juan's
that wraps her. God, she groans, she seems
to worship her seducer!
Mired in the muck of that dream,
I cannot call my motives pure.
I've told you. You just unnerve him.
I'll end it. Then, more of that gold.

RAFAEL
>(As GONZALO)
>Vengeance!
>>(As himself)
>>>A statue just spoke.
>>(As GONZALO)
>>O sir, my bone-tree rots with cold!

OCTAVIO
> Yes, that is how the dead might speak.

(He exits)

RAFAEL
> Hope you all heard him? A just man,
> the Duke, a stern duke, exciting
> as a statue, one who will mean,
> in just, inflexible diction,
> just what he says, and just as
> he said, in stern indignation,
> friends, this just Duke just wants justice.
>> (Music)
> My Ace of Death, help me and sing.
> Mold paste, grind gray stone.
> To play Death is better than to play the King.

(The ACE OF DEATH and the QUEEN OF HEARTS transform RAFAEL into the statue of GONZALO as they sing)

ACE OF DEATH
>> (Sings)
>> *You should a' come,*
>> *you should a' come*
>> *to the feast of them skeleton!*

THE JOKER OF SEVILLE

Papayo! It didn't have no whiskey,
no wine, no brandy, no rum;
they drinking wind, and they singing this: "We
go fête till thy kingdom come!"

ALL
We go fête till thy kingdom come!

ACE OF DEATH
And you will come,
you bound to come
to the bacchanal of the skeleton!

ACE and QUEEN
Papayo! It didn't have no menu,
no recipe you'd ever know,
but the music is bound to send you
to the place we all have to go!
To the place we all have to go!

(RAFAEL *is transformed into* GONZALO. *The troupe exit, singing*)

SCENE 5

CATALINION *enters, carrying a basket.* RIPIO *is hiding, with a knife.* RIPIO *emerges.*

RIPIO
Where's your master?

CATALINION

               Hiding in church.
You're a servant. What do you care?

RIPIO

Save your own soul, Moor; that privileged
olive-oil-tongued, supple-sinewed
son of the serpent has seduced
women for the last time. Come on.

CATALINION

If I'm your prisoner, bring the food.
I'm starved.

RIPIO

              Don't worry. It'll be used.

(*They exit*)

SCENE 6

The cathedral. JUAN, *alone.*

JUAN

Saints, hermits, martyrs! Dreaming stones
with spider webs for irises.
Those sex-starved faces! Everyone's
betrayed the flesh for fantasies.

THE JOKER OF SEVILLE   Act 2 / Scene 6

> When they make a statue of me,
> I hope they'll show this grinding thigh
> damned to exertion, the whole lie,
> the complete man from heel to head.
>   (OCTAVIO *enters as a friar*)
> It's a beautiful cathedral.
> But my mind's clear of all that mist
> of incense. Here you also kill
> your bull on Sundays, and you must
> be the centurion picador
> who pricked him when he cried "I thirst."
> Come, do your necessary business
> before I marry Isabel.
> I'm to be shriven and I was
> always one to please women well.

OCTAVIO

> This way to the confessional.

(*A sound*)

JUAN

> What's that? I heard a woman's voice.

OCTAVIO

> A woman's voice? Well, it's All Souls'.
> Light this candle. This vault is hoarse
> from centuries of cold, there's moss
> in its gullet. Kneel now, confess.

VOICE

> Juan!

Act 2 / Scene 6   THE JOKER OF SEVILLE

JUAN
>That voice! Look, it's a woman
>cowled by the shadow of that arch.
>She signs she'll speak to me alone.
>An assignation here in church!
>Shame! Wait, Father.
>>(JUAN *crosses to the woman—*ISABELLA*—in black, shawled*)
>>>You're a widow?
>You hug the darkness, do you mourn
>for a dead love? Say who you are.

ISABELLA
>No, no. But I implore you, turn
>your head, please. I know that friar
>is waiting for your confession.
>Hear mine: Juan, we lost that garden
>together. We should share its curse
>even if a jealous God harden
>his heart eternally to us.
>My flesh and spirit shine as one.
>No. Do not try to guess my name.
>Ask nothing. I am simply one
>of all your women, whom her shame
>brought joy, even the human bliss
>of damnation with her Adam.
>I have no hope of happiness
>on this earth without you. All I'm
>asking is if you can love. Yes,
>or no. "No" will not change my love,
>but I'm torn by my need to know.

JUAN
>I cannot answer. Not from pride.

ISABELLA
>And I expected nothing less.
>And I am not dissatisfied.
>I love you without bitterness
>and will, even when you're married.
>Goodbye. The friar's curious.

(*She exits.* OCTAVIO *approaches*)

OCTAVIO
>Your body must now be absolved
>before marriage, like a bridegroom,
>while the soul that it should have loved
>alone awaits him in her room.

(JUAN *takes a candle*)

JUAN
>That sky, your painted paradise,
>those dark clouds absorbed my mother
>and brought rain to my father's eyes.
>Since then I have loved no other.
>I've given my life to this question,
>this joke that everybody's heard:
>whether our body's need is sin?
>The One who knows it says no word.
>I'll have a legendary name
>beyond this life. Look, your saints
>were candles eaten down by flame
>to nothing, who went up in smoke;
>wax, and then air! But we are still
>issued bodies to enact one joke.
>Well, mine is burning with a will

Act 2 / Scene 6 THE JOKER OF SEVILLE

    older than death, and older than
    the flame-tipped spires of Seville,
    till it's a candle stub again.
    We're wasting time. I can't light this.
    Bless me, man, in my body's name!

OCTAVIO

    You must be in a state of grace,
    and know the penitence of shame,
    or not marry. Our principles . . .

JUAN

    The rose breathes: "Smell me," the virgin:
    "Teach me," the cling peach: "Eat me."
    "It's you or me," says the scorpion.
    I obey. Isn't that piety?
    I serve one principle! That of
    the generating earth whose laws
    compel the loping lion to move
    toward the fallow lioness,
    who in this second embodied
    his buckling stagger! I
    fought for that freedom delivered
    after Eden. If I defy
    your principles because I served
    nature, that was chivalry
    less unnatural than your own.

OCTAVIO

    Nature produce the scorpion
    as well as the rose; that doesn't mean
    that I should nestle a scorpion

THE JOKER OF SEVILLE   Act 2 / Scene 6

  in my shirt. There are vicious men
  and noble; there's a difference
  between majesty and vermin.

JUAN
  Vermin? No. I remain a Prince
  of Spain, but I can laugh because
  your kind of mildewed, moldering
  chivalry suits a place like this.
  Which is God's tomb, not mine.

(GONZALO's *statue enters*)

GONZALO
  Mine!

OCTAVIO
               Nomine Patris! Look, knight!

(JUAN *turns.* OCTAVIO *withdraws*)

GONZALO
  I've come to supper.

JUAN
                    Oh, fine, fine!
  But, sir, you've caught me unprepared.
  I've just sent out my servant for
  some bread and wine. You know you scared
  that priest? He was my confessor.
  Well, where shall we sit? By this tomb?
  You see, sir, when you didn't answer,
  I took it that you couldn't come.

Act 2 / Scene 6   THE JOKER OF SEVILLE

GONZALO
Stare in these alabaster eyes
when you speak to me. You're afraid?

JUAN
No. You'll recall those courtesies
the living always paid the dead.

GONZALO
I'm waiting sir. Where is my place?

JUAN
Oh, here, this tomb.

GONZALO
No. Keep back, please!
My soul moves by the light of grace.
My body is extinct, my eyes
blown out. All human warmth has gone
from me but rage; and this rage is
the furnace that cast me in stone.

JUAN
It's hot, isn't it?

GONZALO
I'm cold.

JUAN
Yes.
Well, then, cold crystals of hot sweat
pebble your forehead.

THE JOKER OF SEVILLE   Act 2 / Scene 6

GONZALO
                Joke at this:
Hell is the fire in which I freeze
for swearing vengeance in cold blood,
its contradicting flames of ice
char and preserve me. Now, there's food
and wine by the altar. Drink. Eat.

(JUAN *finds food and wine*)

JUAN
Brought your own, eh? What's for supper?
Red wine. Hope it's not spoiled by heat.
What's here?

GONZALO
                The wine is vinegar.
The food, scorpions. You should begin.

(JUAN *pours wine. He drinks and eats*)

JUAN
To your marble health! Vinegar.
That's what they gave God dying once.
You're a father: what would happen, sir,
if God swore vengeance on his son's
murderers?

GONZALO
                He didn't trick women.
Blasphemer! What is your faith?

JUAN
My faith? The faith of all women.
Woman's religion is love.

141

They will resurrect me again.
Imprisoned by laws, everyone
idealizes a liberator
lying next to lover or husband,
and their dream is my creator.
That's what you men don't understand.
I'm as much a vision as
you are. We both don't exist.

GONZALO

Then what about these creatures?
What are they, then?

(*Three apparitions enter*)

JUAN

                Bodies. A forest.

GONZALO

A forest, everyone a trunk.
Anfriso you killed. Batricio, drunk,
cut his roaring throat in a ditch.
That woman Tisbea you bewitched
to drown her beauty. They will serve you.

ANFRISO

I am Anfriso, fisherman
of New Spain. My body, heavy
with envy, crossed a whole ocean
to seek the knight who murdered me.
That jealousy I called honor.
My punishment is serving him
I owe my noble death. Eat, sir.

Act 2 / Scene 6

TISBEA

> The way life hurts is not in books.
> I am nobody; Tisbea, sir,
> forgotten as the face that looks
> long at itself in quiet water,
> water forgets. I am condemned
> to mirrors now that multiply
> my useless beauty to no end.
> Eat. I remember being happy.

BATRICIO

> This throat without a voice they called
> Batricio turned from his own feast
> into a murderer. What I killed
> is standing in front of you. The fast
> music of the Manzanares
> floated my body with the rain
> to this place, with the other trees.
> Mine was the face in the fountain.
> Eat.

(*Enter* JACK)

JACK

> Boy, girl, girl, boy. They called me Jack.
> I was both in that other life,
> till, in the square that day, your look
> divided me, deep as this knife.

GONZALO

> How's your dinner?

Act 2 / Scene 6   THE JOKER OF SEVILLE

JUAN

>   I've had worse.
> Food isn't my thing. The scorpion's
> damned good. The wine's ridiculous!

GONZALO

> Well, no more ridiculous than
> Whoso lusteth after a woman
> in his heart commiteth . . .

JUAN

> Adultery. The man
> who said that was a bachelor.
> God is a reasonable man.

GONZALO

> Where I inhabit now, señor,
> we do not generally discuss
> the reasonableness of God.
> Are you ready?

JUAN

>   For?

GONZALO

>   To come to Hell.

(JUAN *rises*)

JUAN

> You see here a man born empty,
> with a heart as heavy as yours;
> there's no Hell you could offer me,

THE JOKER OF SEVILLE

sir, that's equal to its horrors.
>   (*Music*)
>   (*Sings*)
> *I'll come! It's best to go down a living lover*
> *than a nasty old man penning his memoirs*
> *of liaisons with duchesses and whores,*
> *a night-capped, shriveling prepuce with bedsores,*
> *toothless and creased with grease, one of those bores*
> *who drool on lechery and its hard luck,*
> *who reminisce on every faded fuck,*
> *page after page to live their fury over,*
> *simpering de Sade and cretinous Casanova!*
>
> *Don Juan Tenorio knows when to retire:*
> *a night like this with its fine sweat of stars,*
> *a laughing tropic night, as this one was,*
> *not marbled into fable like your heroes,*
> *but flesh, with all its blemishes and scars!*
> *His legend is the living air, the wind*
> *that pries the room of every shuttered mind.*
> *Immortal and defiant as desire,*
> *Don Juan Tenorio greets Hell with an equal fire!*

(*Apparitions exit*)

GONZALO

Help me to rise. My body's stone
is heavy. Here, give me your hand.

JUAN

All right, Rafael. The joke is done.
>   (*He extends his hand;* GONZALO *grips it*)
Let go!

Act 2 / Scene 6 THE JOKER OF SEVILLE

GONZALO

  I can't! You must understand,
your hand's locked in an agony
of welding ice. Now, we go down.

JUAN

 Rafael!

GONZALO

  I am Gonzalo, Prince!
I am the statue that you killed.
I am the stone that swore vengeance!

(OCTAVIO *appears*)

JUAN

 Father! I'm burning up with cold.
Octavio, hit it! Break the hands!

OCTAVIO

 Rafael, enough!

(*He grabs* GONZALO)

JUAN

    Come on, quick, man!

OCTAVIO

 This is a thing of real stone.
Gonzalo, spare him. Mercy! Christ!
  (JUAN *falls*)
Who will believe what I have seen?
  (GONZALO *withdraws*)

THE JOKER OF SEVILLE   Act 2 / Scene 6

>   A statue gripped him by the wrist
>   and he falls dead. And there's no sign
>   of struggle on him. Rafael!

(CATALINION *enters. A chant begins inside the cathedral*)

CHORUS
>   *Brevis est amor*
>   *in nostra vita.*
>   *Certis est dolor,*
>   *sed in te, Mater,*
>   *in te, sancta soror,*
>   *crescit felicitas.*

JUAN
>   (Dying)
>   *There! Look! My soul!*
>   *Ascending through the air,*
>   *like smoke from a dead candle slowly flying,*
>   *music my dimming eyes can see and hear.*
>   *In this dark moment everything is clear,*
>   *and I am glad, I am glad to be dying,*
>   *to be dying* . . .

CHORUS
>   *In this life our love is brief.*
>   *And grief is certain.*
>   *But in thee, our mother,*
>   *and your sacred sorrow,*
>   *grows our happiness.*

(JUAN *dies*)

Act 2 / Scene 6   THE JOKER OF SEVILLE

CATALINION
    Master!

OCTAVIO
    Honor demanded what was done,
    what was demanded without hate
    of my equal; for the Christian
    warrior must love his dragon.
        (RAFAEL *enters, removing his makeup*)
    Was it you? Rafael! Did you see?
    The statue pulled him down to hell.

RAFAEL
    True? Ah, well, what a pity,
    when I was ready to come on!

OCTAVIO
    I saw it!

RAFAEL
            You saw your jealousy
    induce delirium. But he's dead
    all right. Say nobody killed him. Well,
    the joke is, we were all cheated.
    Statues can't move, and there's no Hell.

CATALINION
    Joker, you have played your last joke.
    This ox is loosened from his yoke.
    Nobody would believe that you,
    Joker, were tricked by a statue.
    Smile, that I served you with honor
    till honor freed me. I'm gone, sir.

God knows where, as God knows I should
forget you, your advantaged blood
that left me nothing in your will
but a song: "The Joker of Seville."
  (Sings)
Sevilla, a voces me llama
El Burlador, y el mayor
gusto que en mi puede haber
es burlar una mujer
y dejarla sin honor.

(*All enter with candles, led by* KING OF CASTILE, DON DIEGO, ANA, ISABELLA, AMINTA, DE MOTA)

DE MOTA
  There is no suffering more monstrous
  than life without a center. Juan,
  you have been loved by all of us
  here, with a love you couldn't return.

DON DIEGO
  My son.

KING OF CASTILE
      Diego, our sons return
  to their true mother. As our souls
  blaze in a resurrecting dawn,
  we bless these lovers and him, whose
  wedding day was his funeral,
  who helped us consecrate this aisle
  in indivisible marriages.
    Donna Ana to her Marquis;
  Octavio to Isabel.

May his death be, down all the ages,
told by the holy marriage bell.

RAFAEL

How silent all his women were!
All statues, like his murderer.
Custom gave us the natural art
to sing in couplets and depart.
And custom gave us our roles
of those who have danced before us,
and we celebrate their souls
with voices alive in chorus.
Every man's life is a candle
that burns too fast, but, with your leave,
we lit his ritual death and ritual
resurrection on All Souls' Eve.

ACE OF DEATH
   (Sings)
*Now, whether Juan gone down to Hell
or up to Heaven, I cannot tell;
whether he gone down to Hell
or up to Heaven, death will not tell;
but the truest joke he could play
is to come back to us one day,
because if there's resurrection, Death is the Joker:
sans humanité!*

COMPANY

*If there is resurrection, Death is the Joker,
sans humanité!*
   (JUAN *is laid on the tomb. The* QUEEN OF HEARTS *crosses, dancing, to his body, unpins a heart from her corselet, and lays it on his*)

O little red bird,
in your cage of ribs, tremble,
tremble and wait,
and he will come now.
The sky has no gate,
the open air is your temple,
every heart has the right
to its freedom,
every heart has the right to its freedom.

(JUAN's body is borne off by STICKFIGHTERS, followed by the company. Dawn. The empty ring)

O Babylon!

For Norline

Note

The play deals with the life of a small Rastafarian community, squatters on a beach that faces the harbor of Kingston, Jamaica, during Emperor Haile Selassie's visit to that country in 1966. The Rastafari still believe that Selassie is, not was, Jah, the Living God. Their doctrine is non-violent; their faith is Peace and Love. There are few true Rastafari. The action of the play moves between the large luxury lounge or disco of a new hotel and a beach settlement. Ideally, the actors should move the scenery around themselves. This text owes much to Rex Nettleford's book, *Mirror, Mirror*, and to a casual but rewardingly erudite conversation with the Jamaican novelist John Hearne.

Jamaican is a highly melodic language. Rhetorical negatives appear for the music's sake. "The proof of the pudding is in the eating" might become "De proof of the pudding nat ina da eating, den?" So, in trying to seek a combination of the authentic and the universally comprehensible, I found myself at the center of a language poised between defiance and translation, for pure

Jamaican is comprehensible only to Jamaicans. But the promulgation of a national language is as much a part of education now as it is of politics. When I considered that, within that language itself, the Rastafari have created still another for their own nation, I faced another conflict: if the language of the play remained true to the sect, it would have to use the sect's methods of self-protection and total withdrawal. This would require of the playwright not merely a linguistic but a spiritual conversion, a kind of talking in tongues that is, by its hermeticism and its self-possession, defiantly evasive of Babylonian reason.

The Rastafari have invented a grammar and a syntax which immure them from the seductions of Babylon, an oral poetry which requires translation into the language of the oppressor. To translate is to betray. My theater language is, in effect, an adaptation and, for clarity's sake, filtered.

D.W.

Characters

SERGEANT BARKER, *a police detective*

DOLORES HOPE, "DOLLY," *a waitress-dancer, Doxy's friend*

RUDOLPH DAWSON, "RUDE BWOY," *a peanut vender, later an entertainer*

RUFUS JOHNSON, "BROTHER AARON," *an ex-criminal turned woodcarver*

VIRGINIA SMALL, "VIRGIE," *a fruit vender, Sufferer's common-law wife*

PRISCILLA JOHNSON, "SISTER PRISCILLA," *an ex-waitress, Aaron's common-law wife*

PERCIVAL JONES, "SUFFERER," *bottle vender and "Abyssinian veteran"*

SAMUEL HART, "BROTHER SAMUEL," *an ex-criminal, Aaron's partner*

ARNOLD DEWES, *a town planner*

MRS. MELANIE POWERS, *Rehabilitation Committee Chairwoman*

DEACON XERXES DOXY, *a politician, later hotel manager*

MR. GOLDSTEIN, *a lawyer*

PUSHER

MAGISTRATE

CLERK

RASTAFARI BRETHREN

THE FOUR HORSEMEN (*dancers*): EDWIN, ELIJAH, DANIEL, SHADRACH

FOUR DREADLOCKS (*dancers*)

RUDETTES: *Rude Bwoy's back-up dancers; also* WASHERWOMEN *of the settlement*

O Babylon! was first produced on March 19, 1976, by the Trinidad Theatre Workshop, in association with Michael Butler, at the Little Carib Theatre, Port of Spain, Trinidad, with music by Galt MacDermot, choreography by Carol La Chapelle, lighting by John Andrews, scenery and costumes by Richard Montgomery and Derek Walcott, and directed by the author, with the following cast:

SGT. BARKER	Errol Pilgrim
DOLLY	Brenda Hughes
RUDE BWOY DAWSON	Wilbert Holder
AARON	Syd Skipper
VIRGIE	Ermine Wright
PRISCILLA	Norline Metivier
SUFFERER	Anthony Hall
SAMUEL	Winston Goddard
MR. DEWES	Stanley Marshall
MRS. POWERS	Barbra Jensen
DEACON DOXY	Errol Jones
MR. GOLDSTEIN	Pat Flores
EDWIN	Feroz Mohammed
DETECTIVE	Bill Turpin
MAGISTRATE	Lawrence Goldstraw
PUSHERS	Stanley Marshall
	Christopher Pinheiro
2 TOURISTS	Lawrence Goldstraw
	Christopher Pinheiro
RASTAFARI	Anthony McQueen
	Andrew Beddeau
RASTAFARI BRETHREN (Dancers)	Evans Antoine, Bryan Walker, Steve Davis, Trevor Redhead
RUDETTES AND RASTAFARI WOMEN (Dancers)	Noble Douglas, Greer Jones, Oscilla Stewart, Alison Brown, Sandra Richards, Adele Bynoe, Corinne Jones, Jennifer Hobson-Garcia

Orchestra: Wayne Bonaparte (*bass guitar*), Vonrick Maynard (*drums*), Gordon Nathaniel (*lead guitar*), Clive Bradley (*electric piano*), Leonard Sam (*saxophone*)

Act One

PROLOGUE

The stage in darkness until a pale neon sign: CLUB NUMBER ONE, *helps us discern a back alley, by a rising half-moon. Heavy rhythm under. Gun shots. Figures cross, freeze, then exit to the sound of a police siren. By swiveling flashlights and headlamps we see* DOLLY HOPE, *in stage costume, some witnesses, and other dancers: the* RUDETTES. POLICE SERGEANT BARKER *walks up to the witnesses as the siren fades.*

SERGEANT BARKER
    Right, Miss Dolly, tell us what happen.

DOLLY
    Very well, Sergeant.
        (*During* DOLLY'S *story the scrim lights up, and behind it the* RUDETTES. RUDE BWOY, FOUR DREADLOCKS, AARON *in street clothes, and* PRISCILLA *as Electric Gyal dance*)
        (*Sings*)

Act 1 / Prologue   O BABYLON!

That half-moon was rising
from the cement factory
on the troubled waters
of western Kingston,
from the sulphur baths, right
round by Rockleigh Gardens,
like a broken spotlight
on Club Number One.

CHORUS

Dem get Rufus,
Dem drop Rufus,
dem get Rufus Johnson in the back with a gun;
four Dreadlocks upon them motorcycle
hit him in the alley of the Club Number One.

DOLLY

Me'd just finish jivin',
came fe smoke a five, when
I catch Rude Bwoy face
by my cigarette flame.
Then I saw four gunmen
shout: "Where's the ganja, Rudy?"
Rude Bwoy screamed: "God, help me!"
That's when Rufus came.

CHORUS

Dem get Rufus,
dem drop Rufus,
dem get Rufus Johnson in the back with a gun;
four Dreadlocks upon them motorcycle
hit him in the alley of the Club Number One.

O BABYLON! Act 1 / Prologue

DOLLY

*Now Rufus had this razor
that him christened "Mabrak."
Him could make it blaze, sir,
like lightning slice the dark.
But who live by the razor
shall perish by the gun,
and Rufe, him was a dealer
in the streets of Babylon.*

(RUFUS falls. PRISCILLA screams)

CHORUS

*Dem get Rufus,
dem drop Rufus,
dem get Rufus Johnson in the back with a gun;
four Dreadlocks upon them motorcycle
hit him in the alley of the Club Number One.*

(Sirens)

DOLLY

*When them heard your siren
above his woman crying,
dem leapt up 'pon their engines
and left with a roar;
them left poor Rufus lying
by the cement factory
like a bag of cement
on this cold alley floor.*

CHORUS

*Dem get Rufus,
dem drop Rufus,*

Act 1 / Prologue   O BABYLON!

    dem get Rufus Johnson in the back with a gun;
    four Dreadlocks upon them motorcycle
    hit him in the alley of the Club Number One.

DOLLY

    A Rasta-man called Sufferer,
    an old-bottle collector,
    limp into the alley, with
    four next Rasta-man,
    saying: "I-and-I shall hide him
    where the Babylon can't find him.
    Priscilla, stand beside him."
    And them take him in a van.

CHORUS

    Dem get Rufus,
    dem drop Rufus,
    dem get Rufus Johnson in the back with a gun.

SERGEANT BARKER and CHORUS

    Four Dreadlocks upon them motorcycle
    hit him in the alley of the Club Number One.

SERGEANT BARKER

    So, where dem gone?

DOLLY

    Beg you excuse, Sarge,
    me next number just start.

(DOLLY and RUDETTES *exit into club as an overture blares.* SERGEANT BARKER *follows. A* RUDETTE *emerges from the stage door*)

RUDETTE
  (*Shouts into the alley*)
  Rudy! Rude Bwoy! Show start, you coming?

(RUDE BWOY, *in stage costume, emerges, carefully*)

RUDE BWOY
  My second name is Jackass? Or what?

(*Blackout. Music*)

SCENE 1

Dawn begins to define a Rastafari settlement on the rim of Kingston Harbor. A corner of SUFFERER's shack. AARON on a pallet, by lantern light; near him, keeping vigil: PRISCILLA, VIRGIE, SAMUEL, SUFFERER, and the FOUR HORSEMEN with their drums.

FOUR HORSEMEN
  (*Chant softly*)
  Jah is I-and-I salvation,
  Jah shall gather all the nations,
  wide as ocean is his patience
  and deep with wisdom like the sea,
  the secret sea,
  the shining sea of
  Jah love and peace,
  Jah love and peace.

VIRGIE
  Praise God, Priscilla. Him is coming round.

Act 1 / Scene 1   O BABYLON!

AARON

Is traffic that? Or the sound of the sea?

PRISCILLA

Is the sea, Rufus.

SUFFERER

And the salt from that sea
has closed up like eyelids your gaping wounds,
and caused you to dream.

PRISCILLA

Is weeks now you critical.
Sufferer save your life, like you save Rude Bwoy's own.

SUFFERER

I collect broken people like I collect bottles.
And you was a bottle filled with the wrong spirit.
You and Samuel here.

(SAMUEL *steps forward*)

AARON

Is Samuel that?
Dem nearly get us this last time, hey, Sammy?
Me tek you for Rasta.

SAMUEL

Them is good people, Rufus.

AARON

Why you don't cut your hair, and shave your beard?
Me never see you so matty. Me feel ugly too;

O BABYLON! Act 1 / Scene 1

>   bring a scissors and razor, girl, mek me
>   shave off this beard.

SUFFERER
>   Him beard, him locks,
>   dem is not to be cut.

AARON
>   I thank you for me life,
>   but me no Rastafari, sir. Come, Priscilla.

SUFFERER
>   Listen to I, Rufus, is weeks we keep vigil:
>   my wife, the good widow Virginia Small,
>   Ras Daniel, Ras Shadrach, Ras Edwin, Ras Elijah.
>   As your wound close, so your eyes open.
>   If you could straighten your wrong-sided life,
>   what you think you would be?

AARON
>   Me never think, sir.
>   A carver, me suppose. Me good with this hand.
>   In it, Mabrak flashed like black lightning.

SUFFERER
>   Night after night, in that dry delirium,
>   like a man in a desert thirsting for faith,
>   you ramble in a dream, about the four horsemen . . .

FOUR HORSEMEN
>   (*To drumming*)
>   Saying . . . saying—

(AARON *turns around*)

Act 1 / Scene 1   O BABYLON!

SUFFERER

    And four stand behind you. You know what you dream?
    Try, try and remember.

(*Music*)

AARON

    (*Rises, moves toward the beach as the morning light brightens. The* FOUR HORSEMEN *mime his vision*)
    (*Sings*)
I stood on the sand, I saw
black horsemen galloping toward me.
They were all white like the waves
and turbanned, too, like the breakers,
their flags thinning away into spume;
white, white were their snorting horses.
I saw them. It was no dream.
They rode through me,
they came from my home,
as fresh as the waves and older than the sea.

FOUR HORSEMEN

    (*Sing softly*)
Zion a' come,
Zion a' come.

AARON

Rider and breaker, one cry!
I have seen them at a ceremony
of lances, white-robed knights,
I forget the names of our tribes . . .
They are coming! I trembled,
To claim their brothers,
To bring them home,

*Thundering round the edge
of the headland, exploding from sight!
Spears shoot on the edge
of the wave every moonlit night—
The horsemen will keep their pledge,
the Knights of Bornu.*

FOUR HORSEMEN
> (*Speak*)
> Saying, saying, saying, saying . . .
> (*Sing*)
> *Zion d' come,*
> *Zion d' come someday.*

(*Silence. Sound of the sea.* SUFFERER *embraces* AARON)

SUFFERER
> That is I-and-I vision of the Great Return,
> which Jah sent to you. For tongues of fire
> can dance on the hair of the least unknown,
> and that crooked man who Babylon bend
> Jah shall make straight. You shall not eat salt,
> the flesh of the sow, and the sow's litter
> shall to you be obscene; the woman, your sister,
> shall always obey you. You shall believe
> that the Emperor Selassie, Jah Rastafari,
> Lion of Judah and King of Kings, is the one God.

FOUR HORSEMEN
> Saying, saying, saying . . .

SUFFERER
> In him is beauty. In him is wisdom.
> For when Sheba travel to Ethiopia,

Act 1 / Scene 1 O BABYLON!

    her jangling procession on the horizon
    a moving oasis of palms and banners,
    lions in the desert rise up to look.
    She couple with Solomon, and from their seed sprang
    Ras Makonnen, the vine and the fig tree
    of fragrant Zion, Selassie himself.
    Now all which is not Zion is Babylon.
    Surrender your possessions, and those
    you have left you shall share with your Brethren.

AARON

    Since me in hiding from the Babylon, since
    they have put me upon bond, never
    to break their peace, and since
    I owe you my life, brother, I think
    I should pay you that debt.

(*Drumming begins. The rest of the settlement enter.* RASTAFARI *women, other Brethren*)

RASTAFARI

    Saying, saying.

SUFFERER

    That razor shall be turned to a chisel, so
    follow your true calling, which is to carve.
    Give him the chisel, and the cap with three colors
    of Holy Ethiopia; anoint his stubble
    like the beard of Ras Aaron, which is now his name;
    and in the name of the twelve tribes,
    I-and-I make this vow, that when we see Zion,
    this man, once a criminal, shall stand by I side,

first the oil that embalms his locks,
by the prophecy of Ezekiel 5 . . .

(AARON *is anointed; a cap, a chisel, and a three-colored shawl brought*)

RASTAFARI

(Sing)
*My locks are holy,
they were anointed
in the everlasting name of Ras,
strong as the lowly
vines, like the pointed
spears of the armies of the grass.
This vow I've taken
of separation,
no razor shall come 'pon this head . . .*

SUFFERER

*Brethren, take him to the flock,
make him faith be as a rock,
name him Aaron from this day,
and teach him what these colors say.*

(AARON *is given a three-colored tam. Then* SAMUEL *also*)

RASTAFARI

*Green for the pastures of Africa,
yellow for the gold of that country,
red for the church triumphant,
red for the church triumphant!*

(AARON *is given his razor*)

Act 1 / Scene 1   O BABYLON!

SUFFERER

Now make this chisel be
the finger of God,
who touch Adam to life.
(A RASTAFARI *brings in a chunk of wood, holds it before* AARON)
Make flesh out of this wood,
if you would carve it good.
Sing with me, sing with me.

RASTAFARI, AARON, SAMUEL
(*In procession*)
Zion a' come,
Zion a' come,
Zion, Zion, Zion,
Zion a' come someday.

(AARON *and* PRISCILLA *are led to another shack*)

SUFFERER

This is your new home, these are your Brethren.
Walk with Jah.

(*All but* PRISCILLA, AARON, *and* SUFFERER *exit*)

PRISCILLA

I so happy for you, Rufus.

SUFFERER

                       His name is Ras Aaron.

(SUFFERER *exits*)

PRISCILLA
 Aaron? . . .

(AARON *turns toward her. Silence. The lights fade. The sound of the sea rises, and fades*)

SCENE 2

Morning. Months later. The beach shack. AARON *struggling with his carving of the four horsemen.* PRISCILLA *planting. Above the shack is a sign:* NEW ZION CONSTRUCTION COMPANY HOTEL SITE. PRISCILLA *leaves off her planting and watches* AARON.

PRISCILLA
 This ground so sour. Aaron, bring your chisel,
 help me dig up this stone.

AARON
                    Me fine chisel, girl?
 That me convert from a burglar's tool?
 Come, give me that trowel.

PRISCILLA
                    No! you plant,
 and me carve.
   (*She runs off with the chisel*)
 You and this chisel! Bet me throw it in the sea!

Act 1 / Scene 2 O BABYLON!

AARON

And bet I cool you off, Miss Electric Gyal!

(*A chase. He catches her*)

PRISCILLA

Aaron . . .
  (*Music*)
  (*Sings*)
How I love thee, my Aaron, let me tell you now.
Sit still, my Aaron, with your quiet eyes and listen:
I love you like that salt sweat on Adam's brow,
like dew upon the breast of Eve that glisten
when they made love the first time in the garden.

That means to say I love you with my soul,
down to damnation, down to deep as hell.
When you're not here, my heart is a black hole,
and you can break that same heart with your smile . . .

AARON

I love you, then, the same Adam love Eve,
to bear upon his back all mankind grief.
I love you as all men
have since loved women,
that is my love.

PRISCILLA

I feel like Eve, so take me where you will,
when she look back the last time on that hill
to where Eden was lying green and still.

AARON and PRISCILLA
> *And hand in hand, the two of them did move*
> *deeper in the grave wisdom of their love . . .*

PRISCILLA
> *That is our love, Aaron, that is our love . . .*

AARON and PRISCILLA
> *And one and one is one,*
> *and one and one is one,*
> *when it is man and woman,*
> *when is woman and man*
> *is one, is one.*
> *Is one is one.*

(VIRGIE, *carrying a basket, enters. She applauds*)

VIRGIE
> One into one could make three, too; but then,
> love have its own arithmetic.

AARON and PRISCILLA
> Peace and love, Virgie.

VIRGIE
> Yes. Let there be peace while we get ready for war.
> You watching Virginia Small, widow, in battle dress.
> This hat is a relic, the righteous socks
> is a legacy from my late husband, Charlie the Diver;
> the desert boots that ready to march
> in different directions, Sufferer just lend me.
> So I ready for war!

Act 1 / Scene 2 O BABYLON!

PRISCILLA

What war, Virgie?

VIRGIE

Child, there is wars and rumors of wars!
We have no legal right to squat 'pon this beach,
for, as Sufferer say: "Where the Brethren settle,
that ground is Zion." Well, Armageddon reach!
For the Reverend Deacon Doxy and foreign investors
called the New Zion Construction Company
acquire this tender for a luxury hotel.
Yesterday was another eviction notice,
stating if we don't move in the next three days,
excavations will begin. Doxy is their puppet,
me hear them investors have him balls in a grip
even a lickle tighter than your friend, Miss D.

PRISCILLA

(*Laughs*)
Dolly and the Deacon is good friends now?

VIRGIE

Girl, if the moon was a silver bangle,
him would ask God to give her, free.
You should see her these days.

PRISCILLA

That Dolly could hustle.

AARON

And as for that John Crow, the Reverend Doxy,
tell him me say "Fly!" We not squatters, Virgie.
"The earth is the Lord's and the fullness thereof."

O BABYLON! Act 1 / Scene 2

VIRGIE
Then is Deacon own too, 'cause 'im is on earth,
and him full of the Lord.

AARON
Is no joke, Mrs. V.!

PRISCILLA
Why them cyan't leave poor people in peace?

AARON
Yes! "War" is right. 'Cause when me look 'cross
that wind-bright harbor and see their big sign:
NEW ZION CONSTRUCTION COMPANY,
me feel to put all Babylon to the torch!
And Samuel in jail now for breaking him bond.

VIRGIE
Well, just make them try and muscle in, me dear,
into the Happy Native Venders Association!
Me not only chairwoman but karate instructor.
Violence is rampant! Life is a struggle!
   (*A shrill steam whistle, then a bicycle bell off*)
O God!

PRISCILLA
Well, your first struggle
for the day reach. Rude Bwoy is here.

VIRGIE
That sexual cyclist!

(VIRGIE *hides. Enter* RUDE BWOY, *riding and singing in time to his steam whistle*)

Act 1 / Scene 2   O BABYLON!

RUDE BWOY
    (*Sings*)
'Ail Queen o' Sheba, Ethiopia's pride,
lift your 'ead 'igh, you ain't bound to hide,
Come mek me take you for a chariot ride.
    (*He dismounts*)
There he is, folks! The man who save my life!
Morning, Brother Aaron, how the carving them?
Morning, Sister Priscilla.

PRISCILLA

                      Morning, Rude Bwoy.

AARON

Morning, God's Messenger! What bad news you bring?

RUDE BWOY

Good news, brother! Me write a next song
and it bad, bad! Me and Dolly break it in
in the club last night. Didn't I hear the voice
of my Ethiop Queen, the Merry Widow Small?
Me feel for a lickle feel.

(VIRGIE *changes her hiding place*)

PRISCILLA

                      She not here, Rude Bwoy.

AARON

You only come around here to hustle the weed
and rip off we doctrine, but you so openly bad,
Rude Bwoy, you almost good. When you go change
your wicked ways, brother?

O BABYLON! Act 1 / Scene 2

RUDE BWOY
> You retire, Rufus,
> me just beginning. Let me stay corrupt.
> Me free and foot-loose. Me don't have a soul.
> When we make a big pile back in Babylon,
> me promise to help you. *Hey, everybody!*
> *God's Messenger reach! Come on!*
>   (*The settlement crowd run on.* VIRGIE *is hiding*)
> God Messenger reach! Capitalism on wheels!
> Business! Business before the big news!
>   (*He deals with his customers*)
> Ha! One flywheel for Brother Edwin's rocket!
> Pack of tomato seeds for sweet Sister Priscilla,
> lickle grass money for my brothers the Horsemen,
>   (*Discovers* VIRGIE)
> and there's my dusky queen!
> Come here, you late love of me young life!

PRISCILLA
> Mind Sufferer don't catch you.

RUDE BWOY
> 'Im is an idler. More mouth than strength.
> Keep your eye out for that one-eye fool!
> Him a' dig out him own eye,
> fe get Veteran Compensation.
>   (*He grabs* VIRGIE. *Music. They dance, the crowd applauding*)
>   (*Sings*)
> *Boonoonoonoos woman!*
> *Sweet cherry soda!*
> *Hot patty and peanuts*
> *and Diet-Rite Cola,*
> *Oh you mek me feel randy,*

saltfish and akee,
strong as sugar-cane brandy,
shake your hurricane bambsy.
Oh my, I want to, yes, oh yes!
Oh my! I want to . . . yes.

CHORUS

   (Singing and dancing)
   Oh my! I want to, yes, oh yes!
   Oh my! I want to, yes.

RUDE BWOY

You the soul of Jamaica,
yes, Mrs. V.
Let me travel your country,
sweet sweet and pretty country,
till I get to Fern Gully,
where it cool and wet.
Get ready, get set!

CHORUS, VIRGIE, RUDE BWOY

Oh my, I want to, yes! Oh yes,
Oh my, I want to, yes!

(SUFFERER, pushing his cart full of bottles, enters, unnoticed, and watches the dancing. The crowd falls back, leaving RUDE BWOY and VIRGIE to dance by themselves. SUFFERER withdraws a bottle carefully)

RUDE BWOY

When me look in your dark eyes,
what do I see?
Poom-poom paradise,
mountain country,

O BABYLON! Act 1 / Scene 2

oh my!
I want to, yes! Oh yes!

CHORUS
Oh my! I want to, yes!

(SUFFERER *ironically leads the applause*)

SUFFERER
Soon as all you finish, let me know.

(VIRGIE *rushes over to* SUFFERER)

VIRGIE
Percy, have mercy! Cage your wrath, tiger.

RUDE BWOY
Mornin', General! Any news from the front?

SUFFERER
All the news seem to be behind my back.
You back-yard stealer of a widow's virginity.
You peanut!

VIRGIE
         Percy, why you so jealous?

SUFFERER
Man mortal, man mortal. See here, Rude Bwoy,
this wound I get fighting Mussolini
in the ranks of Ethiopia, me no field nigger
but a warrior fallen on peacetime. Look!
See this long-service medal?

Act 1 / Scene 2   O BABYLON!

RUDE BWOY

                    Long-service medal, what!
Him was a waiter in the Ethiopian Army
and him take long to serve.

AARON

                    Rude Bwoy, behave!

VIRGIE

Him gwine maim you!

RUDE BWOY

                    Nah. Him love me too much!
This sweet-sweet soldier, this Coca-Cola colonel,
this cork-hat commander of Ethiopia's bottalions,
whose bottle cry is "Peace and Love"?
Him is merciful to the fleas that sleep in his beard.
Come kiss me, General . . .

SUFFERER

                    Go way, batty-man!
   (*To* VIRGIE)
I feel like Moses did, when him come down the mountain
to see you, Mrs. Small, and you, like Babylonians
dancing, idolatarizing the Golden Calf.

VIRGIE

   (*Showing her leg*)
My calf not golden, it brown and it firm,
And it young enough to bruk a lickle dance!

SUFFERER

   (*Roars*)
Dance, Mrs. Small, when your Emperor come
right here to Jamaica! Selassie himself!

O BABYLON! Act 1 / Scene 2

CROWD

What? Here? Him coming? Jah? etc.

RUDE BWOY

You locally assembled Sammy Davis.
You spoil me whole number. It I
who is God's Messenger! Not you!

SUFFERER

Cho! go pump your bicycle! And there is more news.
It just come over the radio, official-true!
Three hundred Brethren will be chosen
for repatriation, for the Great Return.
About twenty from here, no doubt.
Deacon Doxy soon come and make it official.
Now, dance to that!

AARON

(*Holding* PRISCILLA)
                  Priscilla! You hear?
Put your head on my heart, sister.
It feel like horsemen galloping.

RUDE BWOY

How this lickle black man could be God?

SUFFERER

(*Shouts*)
We tried tell you, but your heart deaf!
I shall tell you again why Selassie is God.
It is the coming of the prophecy, Revelation 5:
"Who is worthy to open the Book?" "Answer:
The Lion of Judah, the Root of David.

Act 1 / Scene 2   O BABYLON!

And I saw the Beast and the Kings of the Earth
and their armies gathered together to make war
against him that sat on the horse,
against his army."

RUDE BWOY

                    'Im coming by plane!

AARON

Howell and Reverend Hibbert, Bedward and Garvey.
Reverend Hibbert first preach Selassie was God.
The living God, at Redemption Market.
Howell: jail two years for sedition.
Garvey: jail. I have been in high company.

SUFFERER

And Marcus Garvey was the second prophet,
and him dead, broken; what was his seed?
Universal Negro Improvement Association
back in America. "One God. One Aim, One Destiny."
In the flag of Ghana, that star in the center
is of the Garvey dream of "The Black Star Line."

RUDE BWOY

To me that emblem of Marcus Garvey
is a personal message to Rude Bwoy Dawson:
Be a Big Black Reggae Star. Then them respect you.
Hold on, Brethren. I have a vision!
   (*Music*)
   (*Sings*)
I see the banners and the drums
and the Brethren waving palms,

O BABYLON! Act 1 / Scene 2

babies in their mothers' arms,
in the ghettos and the slums,
when the lickle Emperor comes
to we country,
to we country.
Se-la-ssie a' come,
Se-la-ssie a' come.

CHORUS
(They enact the arrival of Selassie, with SUFFERER as the Emperor, VIRGIE as the Empress, drums, robes, banners, palms. A triumphal dance)
Selassie a' come.
Selassie a' come.

RUDE BWOY
So when the mighty lickle Emperor ask you who
compose this welcome that you sing,
You lift your head and you reply:
Say is a peanut vender born in August Town,
your Messenger, God! Alias Rude Bwoy,
and in him pride and joy him write this song
that we are singing, ooh-ooh!

CHORUS
Selassie a' come.
Selassie a' come.

RUDE BWOY
So when the mighty lickle Emperor ask you who
compose this welcome that you sing,
you lift your head and you reply:
Say is a peanut vender born in August Town,
your Messenger, God! Alias Rude Bwoy,

Act 1 / Scene 2   O BABYLON!

*and in him pride and joy him write this song
that we are singing, oohoo.*

CHORUS

*Selassie a' come.
Selassie a' come.*

(Silence. SAMUEL has returned from prison. He pauses, removes his cap. Hair close-cropped)

SAMUEL

Make him come, Rude Bwoy. But him coming in vain.
Things will not change.

PRISCILLA

     Who is that? Samuel?
Look, Samuel come from prison
with 'im head clean-clean.

SUFFERER

Samuel? My son, my brother?
Lord, him as bald as a baby backside.
Samuel, whose locks was like knotted lightning
that shook like the angry Assyrian kings',
who humble your pride?

SAMUEL

     Them Babylon make me
a clean-face man. Is one particular sergeant.
Him is a Christian.

RUDE BWOY

    Then send him to Heaven.

SUFFERER
    Keep back, Rude Bwoy! This is no joke.

AARON
    Three months ago, Lord, me'd a kill him!

SAMUEL
    You alone? Him mock my conversion,
    we must not eat pork, but him cram the flesh
    of the obscene beast down my craw, then
    him bring out a scissors as them manacle me,
    say, "Your Emperor is coming," and begin to cut,
        (*Music*)
    and as my hair heap up at my foot,
    I sang our creed inside me, so them could not hear.

CHORUS
      (*Sings*)
My locks are holy,
they were anointed
in the everlasting name of Ras.

Strong as the lowly
vines, like the pointed
spears of the armies of the grass.

This vow I've taken
of separation,
no razor shall come 'pon this head.

(**AARON** *smashes a bucket down in anger. Silence*)

Act 1 / Scene 2   O BABYLON!

AARON

>Me cyan't follow how oonoo could sit still
and let the Babylon them walk over you, man!
Cho! Don't you is man, and don't man have fe fight
for him true nature like an animal sometimes?
No man have three cheeks, y'hear? So far, Samuel,
I been calm, and I understand, but . . .
>>(Music)
>>(Sings)
>*All of you know I was*
>*a man of anger,*
>*I was a walking bomb.*
>*To touch me, it was danger.*
>*My head like a grenade,*
>*my body a clenched fist.*
>*My nerves electric wire*
>*against that city: Dread!*

CHORUS

>*Dread!*

AARON

>*Then you opened the book, Sufferer,*
>*to Samuel and to me;*
>*and I bathed in the book.*
>*I lie and cooled my wrath*
>*in the pasture and the brook.*
>*I turned to a man of peace,*
>*my head stay cool as stone,*
>*my fingers like palm trees,*
>*my life was a temple,*
>*my nerves like flowering leaves . . .*

O BABYLON!   Act 1 / Scene 2

CHORUS
Yes, oh yes!

AARON
Nothing could possess me,
I abandoned possession.
I shall come out again,
carrying not peace but a sword.
My tongue shall be a flame,
a bomb in every word.
Once again let me become
a man of anger,
a walking anger,
a restless anger . . .

(Rhythm under)

SHADRACH
Yes. Me say burn it, destroy Babylon now!

CROWD
Yes! No. That is not our way. Burn it. No!

SUFFERER
So, all I-and-I teaching was all in vain?
How often I tell you this would happen?
That your conversion would be put to the test?
Samuel and Aaron, go tell the farthest camp
of the mountain Brethren: the high camp at Pinnacle.
You Four Horsemen, gallop like thunder,
you must reach Negril before the next wave.
Me and Mrs. Small shall travel down the sea coast

Act 1 / Scene 2   O BABYLON!

that faces our exile, till in two days' time,
man, woman, and child shall greet Jah himself
with our single cry.

CHORUS
Only Jah, Jah, Jah,
only Jah can make
Jamaica, Jamaica;
then Babylon will break.

(SUFFERER *embraces* AARON *and* SAMUEL)

SUFFERER
Rufus Johnson, run,
run, but you run toward your name.
Samuel Hart, you run,
for you it was the same.

CHORUS
Only Jah, Jah, Jah,
only Jah can make
Jamaica, Jamaica;
go tell this country wake!

SUFFERER
Ethiopia, hold on,
Ethiopia, hold on.
Jamaica send battalions,
her thirty thousand son.
Ethiopia, hold on!

(RUDE BWOY *leaps onto a box as they circle him*)

RUDE BWOY
*Will be the same way when Rude Bwoy Dawson,
born in obscurity, arrive in New York,
dream city of neon, beautiful Babylon,
greet Rude Bwoy Dawson, Africa true son,
but hear the song den.
Madison Square Garden . . .*

CHORUS
Hold on!

RUDE BWOY
Fillmore East . . .

CHORUS
Hold on!

RUDE BWOY
Felt Forum . . .

CHORUS
Hold on!

RUDE BWOY
*Rude Bwoy Daw-
son soon come,
ten thousand fans . . .*

CHORUS
Hold on!
*Only Jah, Jah, Jah,
only Jah can make Jamaica*

Jah-maica;
go tell this country wake.

Ethiopia, hold on,
Ethiopia, hold on.
Jamaica send battalions,
her thirty thousand son.
Ethiopia,
hold on!

(All exit except AARON, PRISCILLA, RUDE BWOY)

AARON

Priscilla, me and Samuel gone a' country.
Two days. Don't be lonely. Take care of the carving.
Put away the chisel.

PRISCILLA

Don't leave me, Aaron. It's the first time
and I frighten.

AARON

I must. You coming, Rude Bwoy?

(AARON exits)

RUDE BWOY

Nah, me 'ave a lickle business me want finish first.

(RUDE BWOY approaches PRISCILLA)

PRISCILLA

Eh-eh, Rude Bwoy, don't bother with that.

O BABYLON!

RUDE BWOY
> You should come back in the nightclub.
> You have a big future. Is not me alone.
> Dolly keep saying how much she miss you.

PRISCILLA
> Aaron is my future now.

RUDE BWOY
> To burn out a voice like yours singing hymn
> over a coal pot, that seem a sin to me.
> And a body like that should be in public domain.
>> (*Produces a letter*)
>
> Look, I get a contract to perform in a high-class club
> in New Jersey. Italian impresarios.
> And them want the Rudettes and Electric Gyal.
> Passage paid, everything. Is your big break, girl.
> What them have in Babylon
> you can't get in Trench Town.

PRISCILLA
> Get thee behind me, Rude Bwoy.
> Go away.

RUDE BWOY
> This life not in your nature.
> Me hope you don't regret it.

(A WOMAN, *up from a swim, passes wrapped in a towel.* RUDE BWOY *rides after her*)

PRISCILLA
> Me will never regret it, Rude Bwoy!
> *Never!*

Act 1 / Scene 2   O BABYLON!

    (Music: PRISCILLA alone)
O Aaron, come back soon.
    (Sings)
Yard a' empty,
man a' gone,
lickle cook smoke
climbin' on,
climbin' patient
like a prayer,
yard so empty,
him not here.

When you going to come back, Aaron?
I cyan't eat alone,
every day is like forever,
bread soon taste like stone.

Fire dyin',
food gone cold,
gone like smoke
my arms can't hold;
empty sky
and empty sea,
empty I
and empty me.
    (PRISCILLA cooks, packs up wares. Time passes)
When you going to come back, Aaron,
I cyan't sleep alone.
Hear the clock in my heartbeat saying,
Try to carry on . . .
Yard a' empty,
man a' gone,
lickle cook smoke

*climbin' on,
climbin' patient
like a prayer,
yard so empty,
him not here.*

SCENE 3

The same. DOLLY *enters the yard in elaborate beach clothes. She laughs and applauds* PRISCILLA's *song.*

DOLLY
 The voice still good, Miss Electric Gyal.

(PRISCILLA *turns.* DOLLY *removes sunglasses and hat*)

PRISCILLA
 Dolly? Dolly! But look at you, girl!

(*They embrace, laughing*)

DOLLY
 Lord, you mean Aaron leave me for this?
 Look 'pon poor Priscilla. All this for love?
 Your frock faded so, your hair startled up.
 What you living on, girl? The dry bread of prayer?
 You look so maugre, me feel to cry.

Act 1 / Scene 3

PRISCILLA

Save your tears, girl. The price of salt raise.

DOLLY

But don't Rasta never touch salt?

PRISCILLA

And plenty else. Since the old life dead.

DOLLY

Dolly you telling how the old life dead?
Since you all leave the Club Number One, it
deader than a bishopric. I just drop by
because I know that Rufus is not here,
I mean Brother Aaron.

PRISCILLA

                No. Him gone two days
organize the greeting march for the Emperor.
Selassie coming.

DOLLY

        That lickle ole man?
Me glad him could manage.
  (Pause)

                    Is six months now.
So how Rufus look? Him hair long and matty?
Rufus Johnson, Rasta. Me cyan't believe it.

PRISCILLA

You better believe it.

DOLLY
Rasta smarter than me.
Dem nah want work, so dem call work "Babylon."
Dem twist up de Bible to dem convenience
like was jackass-rope. Ganja illegal,
but fe dem, dear, is Genesis: "The Tree Of Life,
for the healing of nations." Me sorry you and Rufus
have fe hide behind that smokescreen.
And Samuel, him all right?

PRISCILLA
No. Not Samuel.
Your people from Babylon cut off him locks.

DOLLY
My people? Me ent have no people but Dolores Hope.
Since Rufus turn him back on all his friends.

PRISCILLA
Him turn his back, and see what them do him?

DOLLY
But ahead was a promising criminal career.

PRISCILLA
And I spoil it?

DOLLY
All I know, Priscilla,
is that before you come in the Club Number One,
playing a sweet lickle virgin from St. Elizabeth,
me and Rufus Johnson was close like that.
   (*Entwines two fingers*)

Act 1 / Scene 3   O BABYLON!

PRISCILLA

    Look, is months, Dolly. What bring you here now?

DOLLY

    Me'll be frank with you, is no tan me come for,
    the sun pounding the sea into zinc,
    and me done black enough, girl, to add
    to my troubles. Some old friends of Rufus
    would like him to pay back an old debt. You know?
    Use your influence, child. All Rufus must do,
    since he has seen the error of his ways,
    is sign this lickle paper confessing that this place
    deal in ganja and so on. And promise Deacon
    and the New Zion Construction Company
    that you all won't make trouble, and move somewhere else.
    It so hot. Beg you some water, please.

PRISCILLA

    Me whole life abide by Aaron, Dolly.

(PRISCILLA *enters the shack.* DOLLY *walks around, examines the carving*)

DOLLY

    Is your choice, girl. Ah, I see, abstract.
    Is like that painter Pizzicato, eh?
    So this is it. Him was always talking in bed,
    when we two lie down in lovemaking sweat,
    about this, how him would sculpt. Him wanted
    to carve me once, too, in ebony. But I say
    "Ebony?" You don't see my complexion?
    Then is this him carve with now? It pretty . . .

(*Picks up chisel, puts it in her bag.* PRISCILLA *returns with the glass of water*)
O God, them reach!

(*Two* TOURISTS *appear at a distance*)

TOURISTS
Hey! Come along, sugar! Hey, Dolly, come on!

DOLLY
Me pick up them two comedian at the club last night.
Me said you might join us for a lickle swim . . .

FIRST TOURIST
For Christ's sake, Dolly. Just bring her along!

DOLLY
(*Screams*)
Arrivederci or whatever, I coming! Shit!
Dem fighting up themself for poor lickle Dolly.
I envy you all this, girl. Faith, love, peace.
But you understand the life as it is.
Try and convince Rufus to leave this place, hear?
Or take my word for it, there will be trouble.

(DOLLY *moves off*)

PRISCILLA
You know, Dolly, you could change your life, too.

DOLLY
Yes. From that rat's rarse of a club called
Club Number One. But someday, you hear, girl?

Act 1 / Scene 3 O BABYLON!

Right where you standing, Miss Dolores Hope,
in a gown that shine like moonlight on water,
going to be hostess of the New Zion Hotel.

PRISCILLA

You will never change, eh, Dolly?

DOLLY

Me? Me like fe eat, gyal.
    (*Music. Lights dim to a spot, the* RUDETTES *appear in silhouette, and we are back in the club. Music. A dance*)
    (*Sings*)
What make we women go wrong—

RUDETTES

Go wrong, go wrong?

DOLLY

Is de pressure, de pressure, de pressure.

PRISCILLA

When de pressure coming on too strong—

RUDETTES

Too strong, too strong, we—

PRISCILLA

Turn pain to professional pleasure.

DOLLY

Give back measure for measure.
We must store up treasure for a rainy day—

RUDETTES
A rainy—

PRISCILLA
And who call we women of leisure—

DOLLY
Don't know what a price we pay.
We is Babylonian victim—

RUDETTES
Babylonian victim!

DOLLY and PRISCILLA
We is sisters trapped by the system—

RUDETTES
By the system!

DOLLY and PRISCILLA
Have mercy on us, your honors.
Nobody here should judge us,
for we toil and endeavor
in we own way—

RUDETTES
In we own way.

(DOLLY and PRISCILLA rise)

DOLLY
For money is still the root—

PRISCILLA
>   *And each woman must seek her truth—*

DOLLY
>   *While the judge and the prostitute*
>   *both working for pay—*

RUDETTES
>   *Working for pay.*

PRISCILLA
>   *So when any woman go wrong,*
>   *is not for the money and the glory,*
>   *is—*

RUDETTES
>   *De pressure, de pressure, de pressure,*

PRISCILLA
>   *Though you might not agree with this song,*
>   *I have heard them sing it so long,*
>   *it come like an old old story.*

RUDETTES
>   *De pressure, de pressure, de pressure.*

DOLLY and PRISCILLA
>   *Miss Dolly and Miss Priscilla,*
>   *them too is your sister,*
>   *but what make them go wrong?*
>   *What cause them to sing this song?*
>   *Don't judge and say wickedness*
>   *is—*

RUDETTES

De pressure! De pressure! De pressure!

(*Freeze. Blackout. Exit* RUDETTES. *Then lights up on the scene as before*)

DOLLY

Dancing and singing. That is your true life.

PRISCILLA

Go quick, quick, Dolly. Me hear
Aaron and the rest coming back.

DOLLY

Me cyan't say hello? Me's a dog?
Me could bark then: "Hello! Hello!"
Ba-bye, then. See you in the club, girl.

(*Exit. Voices off, growing nearer*)

SCENE 4

The same. PRISCILLA *alone.*

AARON

Priscilla! We home!

(AARON, SUFFERER, SAMUEL, *and* VIRGIE *enter*)

PRISCILLA

                Aaron! God, me was lonely!
Virgie, Samuel. You all look so happy!
You all spread the message?

AARON

Yes! And guess how many will be there to meet him,
when him plane touch down at Kingston Airport?

PRISCILLA

Me cyan't guess . . .

SUFFERER

                Thirty thousand!

PRISCILLA

Thirty thousand? You serious?

(PRISCILLA *embraces* AARON)

SAMUEL

Me never thought it had so many.
If our faith was violence, we could
break Babylon in half.

SUFFERER

But in all our joy, Brethren, remember
that tomorrow them coming with the writ
of eviction. And that is the battle.
Come, woman.

AARON
                Stay with us, Sammy.
    Eat lickle bit.

(VIRGIE, SUFFERER *exit*)

SAMUEL
                Thanks. Me so hungry
    me could eat a horse. In fact, them four horses.

(*Points to the carving.* AARON *and* SAMUEL *laugh*)

AARON
    Bring some food, gyal.

PRISCILLA
    Is very lickle, but Samuel is welcome.

SAMUEL
    Joke me did make.
    Only come back fe collect some things.
    Me leave tonight, after me rest lickle bit.

PRISCILLA
    Where you going, Samuel?

SAMUEL
                Pinnacle.

PRISCILLA
                        Pinnacle?

AARON

    Mountain fever a' catch him. Him only going Pinnacle
till his locks grow full and him faith return.
But up in the mountains him eyes get the same look
as me get with the carving.

SAMUEL

    Was me first time in the country, sister.
Yes. Jamaica is beautiful. The beauty of
me own country tame me, like
you a' tame Aaron.

PRISCILLA

              Me na tame him. Him still
bad temper as before.

(*They laugh*)

AARON

              You go with him, then.

PRISCILLA

    (*Laughs*)
Lord, how 'im jealous. But me glad for you, Samuel.
That you find the good place. Samuel a' country!
Me cyan't believe this. Him like him in love.
What it like, Samuel?

SAMUEL

              Zion exact.
Me and Aaron carry the news of his coming,
and the plans of his welcome to all those blue hills,

to Gordon Town, Newcastle, Castleton, Pinnacle,
till my feet can repeat all Jamaica by heart,
and the higher I climb was the cleaner my soul.
  (*Music*)
  (*Sings*)
*Come with me to the mountains,
me have looked in the dusk
'pon the cities of the plains,
I have seen the blue valleys
from Caymanas to Moneymusk,
and I shall never, ever
come down again,
never come down again.
Me a' catch mountain fever,
that cool mountain fever
in my blood like a river,
in the white-bearded waterfalls.
I have heard the old sages,
every rock calls
to me, like the rock of ages,
come with me to the mountains.*

CHORUS
  (*Distant*)
  *Come with me to the mountains,
  Come with me to the mountains.*

PRISCILLA
  Someday we both come, Samuel.

(SAMUEL *exits*)

AARON

> You could give the dyamn man
> something fe eat. Him is my brother.
> You shame me, woman. Poor Samuel.

PRISCILLA

> Poor Samuel. And what about me, Rufus?
> But you left me starving two days and you
> gone to feed the thirty thousand.

AARON

> Rufus?

PRISCILLA

> Sorry.

AARON

> The Brethren will help you.
> I tired tell you that. But you and your stupid
> Christian country-girl pride.

PRISCILLA

> Me cyan't stand charity. Is not pride. Come, eat.
> Is simply me never learn how to beg.

AARON

> We do not beg in the brotherhood.
> If Samuel stay hungry, then me will stay hungry.
> Anyway, time me do work. I looking for the chisel.
> I tired tell you not to move me tools.

PRISCILLA

> I didn't touch them. You look everywhere?

AARON

But what is this? What is this, Father?
Anybody was here? There was evil here,
I smell its perfume.

PRISCILLA

No. Nobody was here.
The chisel can't lose.

AARON

(*Mocking*)
The chisel can't lose!
I beg you take care of it. But, from the time
I-and-I start carving, you grow jealous of I work
like it was a woman. That chisel was blest,
it was changed like I change. But I suppose
you jealous of that, too. You best find it, yah?

PRISCILLA

Me? What the rarse is this now?

AARON

Ras is the Emperor Haile Selassie,
Lion of Judah. Do not blaspheme him!

PRISCILLA

Sorry. I am very sorry that I blaspheme.
But I don't know what to tell you.

AARON

Tell I what you long want to tell me—
that you want to go back to the life you know.
Or go up to Pinnacle with Samuel there.

Act 1 / Scene 4   O BABYLON!

PRISCILLA
>   (*Screams*)
> I didn't lose the chisel!
> God is kind. Me go look inside!
>   (*She goes in*)
>   (*Sings*)
> *Once I cross, once I cross*
> *over Jordan River,*
> *then the soul my life has lost*
> *will be mine forever.*

(AARON *rushes inside the house. He hits her.* PRISCILLA *runs out of the house, followed by* AARON)

PRISCILLA
>   (*Sobbing*)
> You can't beat me so, man. You want kill the child?

AARON
> I warn you not to sing revival hymn in this place!
> And in front of my temple! I try to teach you
> that that hymn singing is a trap, is part
> of the Babylonian plot to keep we in chains,
> in spiritual chains. You stubborn red bitch!
> You refuse fe understand. And you know why?
> You have the wrong blood in you. You can't shed
> the whiteness of the devil.

PRISCILLA
> Then beat me till I black. My mother was a
> Christian. So she a' raise me.

AARON

> She raise you to sell your flesh
> in all the fleshpots of Kingston, too?

(*Pause*)

PRISCILLA

> Lord, me wish you was Rufus for true! 'Cause
> God knows you treat me gentler as a criminal
> than now, when you "good"! You don't love God.
> You is vex with Him, so you raging with me.
> Me hate you, me hate your dyam Emperor!
> Him is a man, not a God. You leave me starving,
> then you come home with this?

(*She weeps. Music*)

AARON

> (*Sings*)
> *Forgive me, gyal. Forgive my terrible temper.*
> *Forgive my harsh words and my raking the past.*
> *The past is such a strong ghost!*
> *A little bit of wind open the door*
> *of your memory, and your confidence lost,*
> *and all your sins standing there,*
> *right there before you,*
> *a knock on the door,*
> *a sound in the wind,*
> *and all the wrong things you done*
> *that you think was behind*
> *standing there in front you.*
> *Your shadow in the sun*
> *can stand up and accuse you.*

What I have done, I have done,
I shall never abuse you again.
It is I who choose you,
past, future, and all;
I shall die if I lose you.
Let's go in, let us lie down
together. Let us live
and forgive,
Priscilla, Priscilla,
let's start again,
let us start again.

(They go in)

SCENE 5

The same. Afternoon. Silence. Then the impatient tooting of a car horn. Silence. The car horn. Shouts. Then DEWES *and* MRS. POWERS *enter cautiously,* DEWES *carrying plans.*

DEWES

Be careful, Mrs. Powers, these people are armed
with a dangerous doctrine: love.

MRS. POWERS

What'll you do, Mr. Dewes,
defend me with a blueprint? Where's Deacon Doxy?
He's the one who set up this meeting here.

DEWES

He's already elected. Why should he be early?
(*Walks around, then calls*)
Hullo! Hullo? You've researched these people;
how do they say "Hello" in Rastafarian?

MRS. POWERS

They drop the 'h.'

DEWES

I'm not surprised,
they've dropped everything else. Especially work.
Bunch of bloody idlers. Look at this squalor!

MRS. POWERS

Rastas are very fastidious.

DEWES

No!
They're not fast and they're tedious.
(*Shouts*)
'Ello 'ello his hanybody hat 'ome?
(*Silence*)
'Ello 'ello his hanyone hat 'ome?
(*Silence*)
This is a site meeting and there's no one
in sight. Well, Mrs. P., I never waste time.
Now, here are the blueprints I promised Doxy.

(*Kneels, spreads out blueprints.* MRS. POWERS *kneels*)

MRS. POWERS

I don't see any plans that include our agreement
with the New Zion Construction Company!

Where's the settlement with its little bungalows
and a bicycle parked in every garage
that we all agreed to call Rasta-Vista-on-Sea?

DEWES

First things first. The New Zion Company
would prefer these squatters to move on their own;
they're foreign-based, they don't want a bad press,
but you know damned well, for the last six months
bulldozers have been poised to demolish this place.
Now, with Selassie coming, we hope that they'll go.
Over there'll be the marina, the shopping arcade,
the mini-golf links, the tennis courts, there,
the Babylon Lounge, a first-class discotheque
with the best local talent money can buy.

(RUDE BWOY *enters, kneels beside them*)

RUDE BWOY

Your prayer is answered.

MRS. POWERS

Who're you, young man?

RUDE BWOY

(*Whispers*)
Shh! The eyes of I-and-I are upon us.
Shake hands, sister, as we kneel in prayer.
Rude Bwoy Dawson, rising star.

(*All whisper*)

O BABYLON!   Act 1 / Scene 5

MRS. POWERS
                    Melanie Powers
from the Rastafari Rehabilitation Center;
this is the planner, Mr. Arnold Dewes.

(*Complicated whispering, praying, shaking of hands*)

RUDE BWOY
    Pray how do you do, Dewes, what are your plans?

(*Before* DEWES *can reply,* SAMUEL *joins the group, kneels*)

DEWES
    Who're you, may I ask?

SAMUEL
                    You may ask.

DEWES
                              Who're you?

RUDE BWOY
    May I call you Melanie?

MRS. POWERS
                    If you want to.

RUDE BWOY
    What number?

SAMUEL
    Me name Samuel, sar. Destruction worker,
them put me in charge to demolish this place.
You and I suppose fe work hand in hand.

(*They shake hands*)

Act 1 / Scene 5 O BABYLON!

DEWES
 Good. Where shall we begin?

RUDE BWOY
     You like reggae, Melanie?

MRS. POWERS
 Reggie who?

SAMUEL
    Mek we start over here, sah?

DEWES
 Good!

(DEWES *and* SAMUEL *rise, exit*)

MRS. POWERS
  Where're you're off to, Arnold?

RUDE BWOY
 Not Reggie. Reggae. See my card, Melanie.
  (*Proffers a card*)
 Keep me in mind when this new hotel open.

(MRS. POWERS *rises*)

MRS. POWERS
  (*Shouts*)
 Arnold! Arnold! You can't leave me alone!

(*There is a thud and a shout*)

RUDE BWOY
> There are some somewhat violent types here, but . . .
> I am in your power, Mrs. Powers. Your blue
> serge eyes are more arresting than any police.
> Come, mek I take your fine freckled forearm
> and show you the settlement. You frighten?
> Dem won't eat him. Him look too hard.

(RUDE BWOY *rises*)

MRS. POWERS
> I am not frightened. Well, Doxy's always late.
> Where to, young man?

RUDE BWOY
> The first thing is the password, *Peace and Love,*
> mek me hear you.

MRS. POWERS
> Peace and love.

RUDE BWOY
> Shh! Not so vexed. Slow and soft, Melanie.
> Slow and sweet, like you chewing a honeycomb.

MRS. POWERS
> (*Slowly*)
> All right. Peace and Love.

RUDE BWOY
> Good! Now every Rasta
> shall know that you wish the world well.

Act 1 / Scene 5   O BABYLON!

MRS. POWERS
   I do. I do.

RUDE BWOY
   But! If by chance anyone should attack you,
   for them have Dreadlocks who pretend them is Rasta,
   but is plastic Rasta, like them who hold Dewes,
   a cry you must learn is to shout Nyabingi!
   That mean "Help, help, police!"
   Then the Babylon will come running
   and preserve your virginity!

MRS. POWERS
   Nyabingi!

RUDE BWOY
   Shh! Not so loud, Melanie. Now follow I.
   I say "follow I" because in Rasta language
   there is no accusative case. Dem feel not guilty.
   You dig I, Melanie?

MRS. POWERS
   I do. Follow I. Nyabingi!

RUDE BWOY
   Me in show business, you know?
   So, mek I show you my place?

(*They exit*)
(*Music. With improvised instruments,* DOXY *is borne on the shoulders of the* FOUR HORSEMEN. *The settlement greets him, dancing;* SUFFERER *strutting ahead of the group, followed by* AARON, VIRGIE, *and* PRISCILLA)

SUFFERER
  (Sings)
  Ginnal, ginnal, and samfie man,
  What is his name?

CHORUS
  Politician!

SUFFERER
  Crash program and five-year plan.
  Water Authority don't give a dam,
  what them a-call him?

CHORUS
  Politician!

(DOXY, during this, is lowered to the ground and formally introduced to the reception committee)

SUFFERER
  Alligator mouth,
  stinging nettle hand,
  him dry as drought,
  breach-of-promise land.
  From east to west,
  from north to sout',
  him neither fish nor fowl nor man,
  but him rich, rich,
  give him a big hand.

CHORUS
  We please fe meet you, Mr. Politician!

(DOXY shakes hands, kisses babies, etc., signs an autograph)

SUFFERER

Mr. Doxy, Mr. Deacon Doxy . . .

CHORUS

Vote for Mr. Doxy!

SUFFERER

Mister Orthodoxy!
Him is a Rasta by proxy,
one thing that him have is moxy!
If we want to keep we locks, we
must put our votes in the box, we
say, Deacon, we understand!

CHORUS

Though you only get here
once every year,
we know you're a busy, busy man.
'Ow nice to see you, Mr. Politician!

(Cheering, etc. SUFFERER calls for silence)

SUFFERER

You Sons of the Negus Churchical Hosts,
descendants of Solomon's dynasty,
Ethiopians of the Orthodox Coptic Church,
the Reverend Deacon X. Doxy, Member of Parliament,
come bearing tidings!

(More cheering. Silence)

O BABYLON! Act 1 / Scene 5

DEACON DOXY
> Pity me, Brethren, I'm a trapped man,
> a deacon with a dilemma, thanks to you all.
>   (*Notices* AARON)
> Kiss-me-neck! Is that you, Rufus Johnson,
> growing beard, locks, and all? I only hope
> you haven't given up your old life for nothing.

AARON
> Nothing make I happier than having nothing.

DEACON DOXY
> Good! People are so skeptical about converts, Rufus,
> they say you're just hiding here from the law.
> Wait, isn't that what's it . . . Miss Electric Gyal . . .
> Priscilla . . . Priscilla. My good friend Miss Hope
> sends you her love.

PRISCILLA
>   Say me send it back, sir.

SUFFERER
> Deacon . . .

DEACON DOXY
>   Where're Mrs. Powers and Mr. Dewes?

SUFFERER
> They was here, but them gone. The tidings, Deacon.

DEACON DOXY
> Today I'm a sad and a happy man. Listen.
> As you all know, Emperor Selassie,

Act 1 / Scene 5   O BABYLON!

>   Lion of Judah and King of Kings,
>   the Living Jah, is coming next week.
>   In parliament through my special pleading,
>   and because I hold your interest at heart,
>   he's agreed to accept a quota of Rastafari
>   into Holy Ethiopia, after his return!
>   (*Cheering*)
>   Now, your own prophet here, Mr. Percival Jones,
>   submitted a list which I hold in my hand.

SUFFERER

>   All must see Zion. Is not only for some!

(*Cheering*)

DEACON DOXY

>   The quota to Ethiopia is three hundred souls—
>   twenty from here, and Mr. Jones . . .
>   No man over sixty, or with a criminal past.

AARON

>   This mean that Sufferer shall close his eyes
>   in exile in Egypt, never gaze upon Zion;
>   that mean Samuel, and I; but if them brand me criminal,
>   then me shall remain criminal.

SUFFERER

>   Peace and Love, brother.

VIRGIE

>   Percy . . .

SUFFERER
>It matters not, woman.

DEACON DOXY
Where there's a will, there's always a bargain.
I swear to you now, Mr. Percival Jones,
that if you assemble your people and leave.
I'll move Heaven and Earth to see that you go.
Make it a ceremony, a treaty, and sign!

(*Holds up a paper*)

SUFFERER
What? . . .

CHORUS
>Sign, sign, Sufferer, then you can go.

SUFFERER
And leave my Brethren abandoned in Babylon?
While I-and-I suffering remorse in Heaven?
No, Deacon! Heaven is for all the twelve tribes.

DEACON DOXY
You're costing the company thousands of dollars,
don't stand in the way of your country's progress.
There could be violence. Don't you understand?
   (*Music*)
   (*Sings*)
We little nations, we
live in the shadow of
the towers of Babylon, we

have no power, we're
a flower in the shadow of
a mighty banyan tree,
we who were pastoral
are ruled by machines . . .

It's a David and Goliath situation
to face the multinational co-orporation,
and not lose our own honor as a nation,
to turn a compromise to a salvation.
That's it, friends,
that's all it means.

Just think of it like this:
business is business;
grow up, friends, and be wise,
let's strike a compromise,
we can never be great,
don't think you're selling out,
be realistic about
real estate.

Yes, it's the Jonah-in-the-old-whale situation,
it's happening to every little nation.
Cooperate with them big corporation
or else: more poverty, more degradation!
That's it, friends,
that's what it means.

(Pause. AARON watches the disenchantment of the settlement)

AARON
   (*Spoken*)
   It don't go so, Reverend. No. Is:
   (*Sings*)
   An eye for an eye,
   and a tooth for a tooth,
   a lie for a lie,
   till it sound like truth,
   but I-and-I know that Mammon is the root
   in a-Babylon!

CHORUS
   (*Softly*)
   In a-Babylon!

SHADRACH
   So the shack and the slum
   until Zion come
   is far better than
   Babylonian plan,
   where man unto man
   is a beast, not a man,
   in a-Babylon!

(The response grows in volume. A slow dance of defiance begins around DOXY)

CHORUS
   In a-Babylon!

SUFFERER
   Speak! Who say?
   Is a long time we dey,

Act 1 / Scene 5

O BABYLON!

now we saying "No way!"
To a-Babylon!

CHORUS

To a-Babylon!

ELIJAH

I-and-I shall reject
progress and project
as long as Mr. Mammon is them architect.
Every man for himself
with no self-respect
is a-Babylon!

CHORUS

Is a-Babylon!

SUFFERER

Speak! Who say?
Is a long time we dey,
now we saying "No way!"

CHORUS

No, no Babylon!
No Babylon!

AARON

I-and-I shall be poor,
but, in I-and-I pride,
I-and-I rich with more
revelation inside
than who by the law

of Babylon abide,
O Babylon!

CHORUS
O Babylon!
O Babylon!

(*Silence*)

DEACON DOXY
You say you're tired of being poor. I offer you this opportunity, you spit in my face! What the backside all you want?
(*Silence*)
I've been sent as a peace delegate, because these people out there exasperated; every day you delay costs them thousands of dollars, and there's a little mechanized army out there, waiting to invade you, at one signal of my hand. I beg you, before this happens, pick up your belongings now and move out quietly. Move up to the mountains, there's a better view of Ethiopia from up there anyway.
(*Silence*)
All right: the blood of these people is on your head, Mr. Jones, you fifth-rate Selassie! Get out of my way!

(*Exits. Laughter*)

SUFFERER
Me wonder what the backside him mean?

(*Silence*)
(*There is a distant roaring hum*)

AARON
What is that?

Act 1 / Scene 5   O BABYLON!

SUFFERER
>That is not the sea.

(*The roar grows nearer.* SHADRACH *runs and mounts the roof of the shack*)

SHADRACH
>Is four men riding. Is like them who get Aaron
>outside the club that time. Four horsemen riding.
>And them swinging chain. Dreadlock!

(*He scrambles back down*)

SUFFERER
>Scatter, form a ring, leave that gate open.
>There will be no bloodshed, and no revenge, Rufus,
>I know it will be hard. Now, you Four Horsemen,
>make we see your mettle. Them is we brothers.
>We go win this victory with peace and love.
>>(*The roar increases. Drums. Music*)
>>(*Sings*)
>
>*Mek we turn the criminal element*
>*to the beauty of the movement,*
>*show them that Jah is we government.*
>*We nah fighting no civil war. We must show them.*

CHORUS
>*Peace and Love!*

SUFFERER
>*Neither Honda nor Yamaha*
>*can ride us down in Jamaica.*
>*Every black man is we brother.*

O BABYLON! Act 1 / Scene 5

We nah fighting no civil war.
We believe in:

CHORUS
Peace and Love!

(Four DREADLOCKS *roar into the arena on bikes.*

The four motorcyclists, with dark glasses, wild locks, are circling the HORSEMEN. A battle-ballet begins.

The FOUR HORSEMEN split open suddenly, running to the four compass points, then turn.

DANIEL runs toward one of the DREADLOCKS, who charges him on the bike, swinging his chain. DANIEL vaults or somersaults and the cyclist crashes through the wings into the sea.

Another DREADLOCKS, swinging a chain, revs toward SHADRACH, who stands splayed against a fence, then darts aside as the DREADLOCKS crashes)

WOMEN
(Sing)
Neither Honda nor Yamaha
can ride us down in Jamaica.
We nah fighting no civil war.
Every black man is we bredder,
we go teach you—

(The FOUR HORSEMEN *stalk in rhythm toward the two* DREADLOCKS)

HORSEMEN and CHO .US
Peace and Love,
Peace and Love.
(The third DREADLOCKS roars toward the FOUR HORSEMEN, who split apart, and he escapes. The last DREADLOCKS kicks his machine. It stalls. He is in the center of the arena. The crowd advancing in rhythm.

The DREADLOCKS dismounts and backs off from his bicycle.

Act 1 / Scene 5   O BABYLON!

>   The crowd steps nearer and nearer. He backs off. The FOUR
>   HORSEMEN suddenly run forward and embrace him)
>
> *Peace and Love,*
> *Peace and Love!*
>
>   (Music. The DREADLOCKS runs off, and the women push off his
>   cycle)
>
> *Peace,*
> *and Love!*

(*The* FOUR HORSEMEN *leap to center and strike a triumphal pose. Exit.*
MRS. POWERS, *disheveled, runs in, screaming*)

MRS. POWERS
> *Nyabingi! Nyabingi!*

RASTA CHORUS
> *Right on! Melanie!*

(MRS. POWERS *screams. Exits.* RUDE BWOY *enters*)

RUDE BWOY
> Thanks to me, brethren,
> or rather, to I,
> Mrs. Melanie Powers
> a' turn Rasta now.

(*A motorcycle engine offstage revving, then backfiring. All leap*)

SUFFERER
>   (Shouting)
> *Take cover! Dem a' open fire! Take cover!*
> *Mafia shoot-out!*

(*The Rastas take cover.* EDWIN *enters clutching a telegram*)

O BABYLON! Act 1 / Scene 5

EDWIN

Rrr . . . Rrrrrr . . . Rrrrrrr . . . where Rrrrr . . . Rude Bwoy? Telegram come, me sign for it.

(RUDE BWOY *rushes over, grabs and rips open the telegram*)

RUDE BWOY

Him have more Rrr . . . dan de dyamn bicycle.
(*Yelps*)
Edwin, you is truly God Messenger. Me ticket reach!
Selassie coming, Brethren, but me gone!
Me telegram reach! Me telegram reach!
See it here! Rude Bwoy rocket launch!
(*Music*)
(*Sings*)
Tell the Deacon he can holler,
him can turn around him collar,
I am flying where the dollar
grow green on the big apple tree.
Me na care about the spring,
summer don't mean anyt'ing,
as for winter, least of all,
what I love most is the fall
of the dollar from the big apple tree,
the dollar from the big apple tree . . .
Though me gift is heaven-sent,
heaven cannot pay me rent.
Only way fe make a cent
is to seek another country,
where the leaves turn into gold.
Me na care how much it cold,
if me future summon me,
I must do what I am told

Act 1 / Scene 5   O BABYLON!

in the city with the big apple tree . . .
   (All exit, except RUDE BWOY)
   (To audience)
So me leave them all right
to their spiritual fight.
Every man for himself was my law.
So take ten, go outside,
we'll put on the flip side,
come back now, we got lickle more!

(Fadeout)

Act Two

SCENE 1

Spotlight, enter RUDE BWOY *in heavy winter gear, carrying a guitar. Music. Snow is falling.*

RUDE BWOY
O Babylon! Side two. Rhythm track!
Well, me hit the Big Apple in wintertime.
Subway rattle, police sirens, occasional gunfire . . .
   (*Through the scrim: the* RASTAFARIAN *settlement, men and women around their cooking fires on the beach.* AARON *enters and watches the scene from a distance*)
Me could look right through that curtain of flakes,
remembering night fires flickering on that beach.
   (*Sings*)
How beautiful are the Brethren
in their rites of contemplation,
how quiet this congregation of men.

*From the incense writing
their names on the air,
they are slowly transformed;
the rags, the ragged beards and wild hair
transformed to what
through the sweet-smelling smoke they really are* . . .

(*Music under. A black* PUSHER *emerges*)

PUSHER

How you doin', Sunshine? Bring any grass?

RUDE BWOY

Pure Jamaican, bwoy. But a lickle green, first.
Just business, dig?

(*Another* PUSHER *has emerged; he holds a knife against* RUDE BWOY)

SECOND PUSHER

Dig.

(SECOND PUSHER *digs in knife.* FIRST PUSHER *frisks, strips* RUDE BWOY *of money and marijuana*)

FIRST PUSHER

Keep smiling, Sunshine . . .

(*They run off. Music up*)

RUDE BWOY

Well, Rudy Bwoy. Welcome to Babylon.
Every black cent gone . . .

(*The scrim rises. The snow blurs* RUDE BWOY. *The firelight shows* AARON)

AARON
>   (*Sings*)
>   *How beautiful my Brethren*
>   *in their rites of contemplation,*
>   *how quiet this congregation of men!*
>   *Their smoke-chafed eyes*
>   *bulge into garnets, their locks*
>   *are the black wool of wild mountain rams*
>   *that startle the rocks*
>   *with their leaping,*
>   *as this moment embalms*
>   *them with spices and smoke. Look,*
>   *how beautiful are my Brethren!*

(RUDE BWOY's silhouette fading)

RUDE BWOY and **AARON**
>   *How beautiful the murmuring and sleeping*
>   *congregation of Brethren.*
>   *They crouch around fires like warriors of old.*

(PRISCILLA stands in the doorway)

AARON
>   *May my chisel build—*

RUDE BWOY
>   *And my songs gild them—*

AARON and **RUDE BWOY**
>   *To a solid frieze of Abyssinian gold.*
>   *How beautiful my Brethren!*

Act 2 / Scene 1   O BABYLON!

ALL

> *How beautiful my Brethren,*
> *how beautiful my Brethren!*

(RUDE BWOY *exits in falling snow.* AARON *enters the firelit yard*)

PRISCILLA

Aaron, where you been? You look so strange.
Had one big fire in Kingston last night.
Them burn the Zion Construction Company.
What happen? Something heavy a' worry you?
You didn't say where you went.
What is wrong?

AARON

           You ask too many questions, woman.
What is wrong? You heard what Deacon said.
All them that have criminal charge cannot go.
So, me and Samuel . . .

(SUFFERER *approaches*)

PRISCILLA

Them will send you, Aaron. The bond is not forever.
Look Sufferer, him was asking for you all last night.

AARON

How it go, Sufferer?

SUFFERER

          Me old wound a' pinch me.

AARON

Mine don't too much. But yours was in war.

SUFFERER

> You fighting a war same like I, brother.
> How pretty the night stay, eh? Just so the stars
> hang over the great Danakil Desert,
> thicker than medals 'pon Mussolini chest.
> Couldn't find you all night. Where you went?

AARON

> Walking and thinking through the streets of Babylon.

(VIRGIE *enters*)

VIRGIE

> Your man come back, your yard full. You happy, girl?
> Come, Priscilla. Come brush out this old head.
> Pass a lickle Gilead balm 'pon this forehead
> To smooth 'way the worries of the night.

(PRISCILLA *and* VIRGIE *sit apart*)

PRISCILLA

> You never tell me, Virgie. Who was Charlie,
> your first husband? How you come to lose him?

VIRGIE

Charlie? How I lose him? Him tell me one night, when it was hot, "Woman, me think me gone swim." And I say, half-sleep, "Swim, Charlie?" And him laugh: "Is not the middle of the night, look, through the window I see the forehead of the mornin." I say, "Think how cold the water stay then!" and me turn over to snore. Then I hear him packing him suitcase, and I vex: "You going swim with your suitcase, Charlie?" And him laugh again, but sad, you know? "Well, is a long swim, girl." And him gone. After that, 'im could not see the forehead of the morning nor the heel of the evening, for him gone down too deep.

PRISCILLA

You mean him went mad
from waiting for Zion?

VIRGIE

In nineteen hundred and fifty-eight,
Reverend Claudius Henry's Emanuel Brethren
sell three thousand tickets for Ethiopia;
three thousand people choke up the wharf
studying the sea. But boat never come.
So I can imagine how them two must feel.

PRISCILLA

                              Such faith
does frighten me. It don't seem fair
that Sufferer, Aaron, and Samuel can't go
back home to Zion with their Emperor.

VIRGIE

Samuel has found his peace at Pinnacle.

AARON

You all right, Sufferer?

SUFFERER

                      Oh, the old faith rekindle
this one eye again. That can never go out.

AARON

You love Selassie a long time, sir.

(*Music*)

SUFFERER
(*Sings*)
In my youth, in my youth,
there was a beautiful man,
with the face of an eagle
and the soft eyes of a lamb,
(Projections: Selassie at the League of Nations)
that Mussolini, Mussolini take away his land.
Him was a man of peace,
him was a dove of gentleness,
him stand alone upon a box before the League
of Nations.

CHORUS
Upon a box before the League of Nations.

SUFFERER
Him was a spirit
of brotherness,
him was a shining example of my people's patience.
Them take away his country,
they say the dead
was wider than that sea.

CHORUS
Selassie O
Selassie O!

SUFFERER
But that was in my youth,
my youth, my youth.

Nobody hear him voice,
his anguish cry in vain,

Act 2 / Scene 1 O BABYLON!

*and the carrion crow them feast on his people,
days upon days upon days . . .*

CHORUS

*O Ethiopia!
Nobody listen when you cry!*

SUFFERER

*Nobody listen,
nobody hear you as they don't hear I.
But dread and death
is only for time,
they too shall pass
same way that my youth gone.
O Prince of Peace, tell Sufferer you have come
across the ocean and the bitter seas
to take him home.
Give back to me the faith that was my youth,
give back, give back,
give back my Emperor his kingdom . . .*

CHORUS

Peace.

(Silence. Sound of the sea)

SUFFERER

Well, now is the time to confess, me suppose.

AARON

Confess what?

SUFFERER

Oh, that me never
fought in Ethiopia. Never see no strange stars.

O BABYLON! Act 2 / Scene 1

The wound me get in a fight with a carter-man
over a card game, in me roaring youh.

AARON

Me did always guess that. Never mind,
you been like an Emperor to me.

SUFFERER

                          Thanks.
Bottles and all? Rude Bwoy is right.

AARON

                      Bottles and all.
Rude Bwoy love you.

SUFFERER

             You know, me miss him?
Me miss him teasing me with the Widow Small.
Used to make me feel young to be jealous.
Wonder how him doing in America? America.
It is Zion for some. Rude Bwoy, him just gone
to a richer bondage.

AARON

           Maybe him right?
Will we see Zion, Sufferer?

SUFFERER

We shall, brother. Me almost sorry me cause you
to change your life. Maybe a criminal
was more successful.

(*Two* DETECTIVES *appear, one dressed like a Rasta*)

Act 2 / Scene 1   O BABYLON!

SERGEANT BARKER
             So we meet again, Rufus?

AARON
Sergeant Barker, or rather, Barber, since
you cut off me Bredder Samuel locks.
What you want here?

SERGEANT BARKER
                   You under arrest.
   (*Showing the chisel*)
This tool is yours? It initial R.J.

AARON
                         Yes.

SERGEANT BARKER
Cuff him.
   (*The* POLICEMAN *handcuffs* AARON)
   (*To crowd*)
Now you all will have to get out of this place!
You lose it already because of him.

AARON
You bitch!

SERGEANT BARKER
         That's me boy, Rufus!

AARON
What is the charge?

SERGEANT BARKER
              Sedition and arson.
We have a woman witness to prove you was seen

240

O BABYLON! Act 2 / Scene 1

>   loitering around them warehouses last night.
>   You use this chisel to pick them locks
>   like a burglar gemmy. The fire set from inside.
>   We know your methods from long, long time.
>   >   (*To crowd*)
>   You all take him among you and he do you this.
>   How you could change Rufus? It would take a miracle.
>   Me know you'd a' return to that fiery temper
>   like a dry drunk to his waters. Rage is your spirit.
>   Come home, the boys missing you. You identify this?

(*Showing the chisel*)

AARON

>   (*Lifting his hands*)
>   I identify this as the Babylonian captivity
>   that the faithful must suffer before
>   dem see Zion. Best take I in peace, Babylon,
>   if you don't want I raise I-and-I voice
>   and, with one cry, bring riot.

FIRST POLICEMAN

>   That me would like. Come.
>   (PRISCILLA *rushes forward*)
>   This madman is your husband?
>   Him was out all last night?

AARON

>   Answer them, woman.

PRISCILLA

>   Yes, sir. Me never see him last night.
>   All of that is true. But him change!

Act 2 / Scene 1   O BABYLON!

   Him change. Him would never do this!
   Rufus, swear in God's name you never do it!

AARON

   All right, then. I swear by your God, Priscilla,
   that I never do it. Them want frame I.
   You best come in peace, Babylon.

SERGEANT BARKER

   Come, hairy bwoy.

AARON

                    Good. Truth shall prevail,
   I-and-I nah need no lawyer. Priscilla,
   take care of the carving, dem.

(AARON *is hustled off. Music.* PRISCILLA *screams*)

PRISCILLA

   Virgie! Virgie! You see? Them a' take him!

(VIRGIE *restrains* PRISCILLA)

VIRGIE

   (Sings)
   Hold hard, hold on hard, girl,
   bear each blow, every shock,
   is the way of this world.
   Now that rough seas
   will wash you,
   fasten on to his memory
   like the crab grip the rock.
   Don't let go,

don't let go,
don't let go.
   (A chorus of SETTLEMENT WOMEN *joins them*)
You sufferin' now, but
your sorrow will pass
and your cryin' renew you
as the rain the new grass.
Believe me, it's true, true—
every sorrow must pass,
every sorrow must pass.

VIRGIE and CHORUS OF WOMEN
   Don't let go,
   don't let go,
   don't let go!

(*They lead her toward the shack*)

VIRGIE
   See, sometimes the butterfly
   in the battering breeze
   that lick down big trees
   can cling to the leaf
   with the strength that is ease.
   Please, please,
   don't let go.

VIRGIE and CHORUS OF WOMEN
   Don't let go,
   don't let go.

(VIRGIE and PRISCILLA *enter the shack. The lights fade, then go up immediately on*)

SCENE 2

RUDE BWOY's *dressing room.* RUDE BWOY *in outlandish winter gear and a wide hat, primping before a mirror. A knock and the assistant* STAGE MANAGER *comes in.*

STAGE MANAGER
   Letter from home for you, Dawson.

RUDE BWOY
   So you could read, eh? You read *Variety? Downbeat? Jet? Black Stars?* No, you never read that to rarse, but you could read my mail, eh, skinhead? Well, if you used to read, Sonny Boy, you would know by now is either Rude Bwoy or Mr. Dawson. A next thing: several people dropping in with their fly already half open, believing that this is the bathroom, so you better get me a place appropriate to my status, right?

STAGE MANAGER
   All right, Dawson. Band's warming up.

RUDE BWOY
   I glad. Is the only heat in this bumbuh-cloth place.
   Gimme the letter, and *close the door!*
      (STAGE MANAGER *exits.* RUDE BWOY *opens the letter, speaks to the audience*)
   Next thing, I get this letter from the Merry Widow Small.
   Dear Rude Bwoy:

(VIRGIE *enters, dressed for court, followed by* PRISCILLA; *as she speaks the letter, she sets up the court: a bench, a bar, etc.*)

O BABYLON!   *Act 2 / Scene 3*

VIRGIE

    Dear Rude Bwoy: Please send us some money.
    The Brethren need help bad. Plenty things happen since you
    leave, me dear. The Babylon arrest Aaron for arson
    two days before the Emperor come. So we all gone
    to court. Me take Priscilla. Try and imagine it!

SCENE 3

The settlement becomes a courtroom. Characters enter as named.
RUDE BWOY, *apart, watching.*

VIRGIE

    A white magistrate, but him was soft-hearted. We get
    Aaron the best lawyer, a Mr. Goldstein, and everybody
    give evidence. Dewes, Dolly, and all. Your good friend
    Mrs. Powers testiclify—

(MRS. POWERS *on the stand*)

MRS. POWERS

    . . . that when our official committee arrived,
    we were raped, drugged, assaulted, and mocked,
    because of the news of their Emperor's coming,
    as if his arrival permitted such wildness.

(DEWES, *in a hat, rises*)

Act 2 / Scene 3   O BABYLON!

DEWES

> We were not trespassers, we were within our rights,
> it's corporation property. They're squatters,
> so they'll bloody well have to move.

MAGISTRATE

> Sit down, Mr. Dewes. It's your turn next.
> Please step down, Mrs. Powers.
>   (MRS. POWERS *steps down*, DEWES *takes the stand*)
> Remove your hat.

DEWES

>   In one minute. You'll see why.
> Sir, I'm sick and tired of these Brethren, sir!
> They just float around, rootless,
> without any law. They refuse to conform;
> every gesture of progress is called Babylonian
> and is stubbornly resisted, in the extreme.

MAGISTRATE

> I thought their doctrine was pacifist.
> Peace and Love, and so on. They're violent?

DEWES

> Are you saying that this bump on my cranium
> was put there by a pacifist?

(Removes *his hat; his head is bandaged*)

MAGISTRATE

> I see. You may keep your hat on.

O BABYLON! Act 2 / Scene 3

DEWES
> Their leaders
> are two of Kingston's most renowned criminals,
> Rufus Johnson and Samuel Hart.

MRS. POWERS
> Don't forget that little rapist!

(RUDE BWOY *exits*)

DEWES
> Cannibals who get high on cannabis!
> I'd sue them, but they don't believe in money.
> I may be a capitalist, but I'm also a Christian.
> They interpret God's word to their convenience,
> they babble on about Babylon, they lie on
> the Lion of Judah, and the Abyssinia they want
> is an abyss of sloth! It's a smokescreen.
> I want justice, that's all. The law is the law.

MAGISTRATE
> Step down, Mr. Dewes.

(DEWES *sits*)

DEWES
> The law is the law.
> Take my head for a damned egg or what?

MAGISTRATE
> Call the next witness.

CLERK

    Dolores Hope.
Dolores Hope.
 (*Music:* DOLLY *enters*)
    Raise your right hand.
Do you solemnly swear to tell the truth, the whole truth,
and nothing but the truth,
so help you God?

DOLLY

    Cool.

MAGISTRATE

    Beg your pardon, Miss Hope.

DOLLY

 Sorry, sar . . .

GOLDSTEIN

    You may proceed . . .

DOLLY

 Thank you, your honor. Well!
  (*Music*)
  (*Sings*)
 Me d'strolling by Parade
 down by the Ward Theater
 minding me business . . .

GOLDSTEIN
 Which is?

DOLLY

Which is? 'Ow you mean?
Which is taking lickle breeze,
a lickle window-shopping, me ent doing nothing greater
than digging the scene . . .

GOLDSTEIN

When?

DOLLY

When what? Take your time, what happen to you?
Me ent commit no crime.
Well, sar, fe continue:
me a'strolling by Parade
down by Ward Theater
minding me business,
waitress is my business,
just catching lickle breeze,
a lickle window-shopping, just doing nothing greater
than digging the scene.
Me was demonstrating nothing, me ain't no demonstrator
like them washing machine.

GOLDSTEIN

Washing machine?

DOLLY

Sah, I was checking on the price of
dem washing machine.

CHORUS

She was checking on the price of
dem washing machine.

GOLDSTEIN
> Go on.

DOLLY
> Well, I notice that man
> into the shadow of the theater
> when a car light pass on . . .

GOLDSTEIN
> You're sure it's this person?

DOLLY
> Sah, when the car lights pass on
> this person in person,
> I see him quite clear and I see him was one
> of them radical, madical, rank agitator!

GOLDSTEIN
> You can't make allegations.

DOLLY
> Alligator, me rarse!
> Me ent no damn alligator!
> I find you dyam fast,
> is him that I see,
> swear to God, my creator!
> Is this man that I see,
> strolling round by Parade,
> round by Ward Theater.
> Is him who raise arson
> as me went window-shopping
> for me washing machine.

*Nobody 'a bribe me
with no washing machine.*

(*Exits*)

MAGISTRATE

We have heard all the witnesses for the prosecution. Now, let's
hear from you, Mr. Goldstein. Let the accused come forward.
  (AARON *is brought out*)
I've looked at your record. You've a fearful number
of previous convictions, Mr. Johnson.
Assault, three armed robberies, drug trafficking.
Another assault. And now this: arson.

AARON

Me say I-and-I change, sah.
  (*The court laughs*)
              Hyena
does laugh at lion, but him never come close!
Me not saying, sir, me begin complete.
But as I see the kindness and poverty of my Brethren,
my faith start fe grow with my beard and my locks.
  (*Music*)
*Some evenings I would look out on the sea, walk by the water, I
would turn around and I would see all the shacks and hovels,
all the garbage and the filth, and the sore-foot pickney and the
women dry and black like burnt cane. And the hot-oven gully,
and the dust so thick in the throat of the leaves they can't talk
any more, and the Brethren eyes red from the smoke of the
weed, and, above all the shacks, like high priests, the black
crows . . . just 'pon that second before the sun sink and the
moon enamel everything silver, I see the Holy City. I see it
right here, and is not Babylon I saw, but Jerusalem, Jerusalem,
that is all.*

Act 2 / Scene 3   O BABYLON!

RASTAFARI

Amen, amen, saying, saying . . .

AARON

And Rufus rise, a changed man! But the Babylon
never believe I, or I brother Ras Samuel.
Me thank Mr. Goldstein deep for him efforts,
and for once in she life, Dolly talk the truth.
  (PRISCILLA *rises*)
Revelations say, as Sufferer instruct:
"The kings of the earth, when they see her burning,
shall cry woe to Babylon! That mighty city!"
I acted by prophecy. That is a sin, then?

MAGISTRATE

Is that what you taught him, Percival Jones?

SUFFERER

I teach no violence. It is his temper, for
where him live on that beach was like paradise, sir.

AARON

Is who Jamaica must belong to, sah?
That angel who mark his X 'pon our doors
from the New Zion Construction Company,
him is Babylon bailiff. But, never mind, sar.
From the angry of this earth, more fire must come.

MAGISTRATE

You're not the one to set it, Johnson.

AARON
>Who can say, sar?
>>(*Turns to* PRISCILLA *and* SUFFERER)
>>>Sufferer, I sorry.
>Priscilla, me went walking late last night,
>thinking how our conversion was of no use.
>I was in rage at what them do, Samuel.
>I wept that I name was not among the chosen,
>and me burn down the New Zion Construction Company.

PRISCILLA
>You lie to me! You lie to me! Rufus! Rufus!

(PRISCILLA *rushes out, followed by* VIRGIE *and* SUFFERER)

AARON
>Go then, go! Thou Whore of Babylon!

(AARON *screams in despair*)

MAGISTRATE
>Restrain him! You must keep your temper here, sir!
>We've heard all the evidence; now, Mr. Goldstein,
>before I pass sentence, is there anything else?

GOLDSTEIN
>Sir, the crime of poverty, to which the world is a witness.
>Sir—
>>(*Music*)
>>(*Sings*)
>*We do not have, we do not need a witness*
>*to the history of injustice*
>*of the world outside these windows.*
>*Therefore, your honor, our defense is simply this:*

*Oh who in his heart has not wanted to burn
the unjust city?
The ghettos, the slums, the barrios, the dunghills,
the shanty-towns, Laventilles, Harlems,
from Rio to Kingston?
Who has not raged like a fire,
when all a great fire needs
is one spark of pity?
Who would not have the city of our desire
instead of these dunghills of shame?
And if that destruction is just,
where does such a holocaust start?
In the heart that burns like a simple flame.*

*We are all murderers,
we are all destroyers:
the criminals that we defend
and the criminals who defend us, the lawyers;
if you believe in his dream,
redeem him.
If you would perpetuate the ghettos, the slums, the
barrios, the dunghills, the shanty-towns, Laventilles,
Harlems,
from Rio to Kingston, condemn him!
But if we who are the just
lock him up in darkness,
I know, in the depth of that dark,
you will still see something burning,
starlike, a diamond, unquenchable,
a simple spark!*

MAGISTRATE

Rufus Johnson, also known as Ras Aaron,
I believe you've tried to change your life.

I shall try to be as lenient as possible.
You are guilty of arson, a serious crime.
The Zion Construction Company says
it will waive damages if your people move.
So because I don't wish to provoke your people,
thirty thousand of whom serenely await
your Emperor's coming, you're denied the privilege
of seeing your Emperor in serving three months' hard labor
in Spanish Town prison, and after that,
you are once more bound over
to keep the peace.

(*Exits.* AARON *is being taken away by two policemen*)

AARON

           You mean I shall not see Him?
Then no! No, my lord, I cannot keep the peace
no more. For month upon month
I kept my temper. But now, let the horsemen come!
I break my bond. I hereby break my bond!
For a raging Rasta is Armageddon's angel!
    (*A Rasta war dance begins. Armageddon*)
    (*Sings*)
The lightning was black!

CHORUS
    Mabrak!

AARON
    And white was the night!

CHORUS
    Mabrak!

Act 2 / Scene 3

AARON
> *As the blind man see!*
> *I saw with no sight!*

CHORUS
> *Mabrak!*

AARON
> *So I John saw.*

CHORUS
> *What you saw?*

AARON
> *I saw the rich of this earth—*

CHORUS
> *Mabrak!*

AARON
> *On their knees eating grass—*

CHORUS
> *Mabrak!*

AARON
> *In the Babylonian wilderness*
> *Like the King Nebuchadnezzar.*

CHORUS
> *Mabrak!*

AARON
New York, London, Babylon,
this shall come to pass.

CHORUS
Tell it!

AARON
I John saw,
I John saw!

CHORUS
O Zion!

AARON
I saw the Whore of Babylon
in scales of green and gold.

CHORUS
Mabrak!

(PRISCILLA emerges as the Whore of Babylon: Electric Gyal)

AARON
Her lips was red as fire,
but her flesh was cold.

CHORUS
Deliver him!

AARON
I saw every city
in its shirt of fire—

CHORUS
> *Fire!*

AARON
> *And that woman laugh in pity—*

CHORUS
> *Mabrak!*

AARON
> *At the living man called I.*
>> (The RASTAFARIANS as Masai warriors and spearmen)
>
> *And those who stooped low—*

CHORUS
> *Mabrak!*
> *Nyabingi!*

AARON
> *Beaten out of all pride—*

CHORUS
> *Nyabingi!*
> *Mabrak!*

AARON
> *In Babylonian woe,*
> *them all straighten their back—*

CHORUS
> *And them shake their dread hair*

AARON

And them fit what they were—

CHORUS

Nyabingi!
Mabrak!

AARON

(*Draws bow*)
As the arrow fit the bow!

(*Dance: series of leaping archers*)

CHORUS

Nyabingi
Mabrak!

AARON

As the hand fit the spear!
And the Lion his hide!

CHORUS

Nyabingi!
Mabrak!

AARON

As this living body—

CHORUS

Mabrak!

AARON

Fit my soul like a glove—

Act 2 / Scene 3

CHORUS
Mabrak!

AARON
Let the doctrine of love—

CHORUS
Nyabingi
Mabrak!

AARON
Turn to fire and war!
like a falcon, the dove.

CHORUS
Mabrak!
Nyabingi!

AARON
For once I loved this world,
but this world don't want love.

CHORUS
Nyabingi
Mabrak!

AARON
What this world love most is war! War! War! War!

CHORUS
Nyabingi!
Mabrak!

AARON
(Faster)
And then I saw nothing
and nothing again,
and my life turn nothing
and I bleed in vain
and I called to my people
in my distress,
and my people cry answer
and their cry was:
Yes, yes! No mind if you suffer,
cry yes! Yes! Yes!

(The jail doors descend and slam down before him. The sky is afire. The apparitions vanish)

SCENE 4

The settlement, partially demolished. A sign is lowered: NEW ZION CONSTRUCTION COMPANY RIBBON CUTTING CEREMONY. *A ribbon strung across the site. Workmen. Music. Enter* DOLLY, DOXY, DEWES, MRS. POWERS.

DEWES
Yes. Let's thank God, Deacon Doxy,
that by next week these hovels will vanish
like a nightmare, and these people will learn
to lead decent, Godless, respectable lives
like everyone else.

MRS. POWERS

                Yes, Mr. Dewes.
It's time to cut the umbilical cord
that joins them to Zion. The scissors, Miss Hope.

(*She proffers scissors to* DOLLY *to cut the ribbon.* DOLLY *hesitates, then sobs*)

DOLLY

    (Weeping)
Yes. Yes. Well, yes. Yes. So, we succeed, then.

DEACON DOXY

    It's progress, Dolores, and it hurts.
But it's for the ultimate good.

MRS. POWERS

    If they want to build Jerusalem, let them
get off their arses and lift a bloody shovel!

(*Music. During this number, we see the shacks being torn down by the* DREADLOCKS *in hard-hats and overalls, as the dinosaur shadow of a steam shovel rises and falls*)

DEACON DOXY

    (Sings)
Don't tell me about Zion,
I've got work to do.
Call me a con man, just the usual lying
politician. The Zion I'm building
is schools for their children,
a place in this world,
and I'm trying to build it for them and for you.

DEWES
*In the ideal republic there's no need for visions,
and what are their visions?
A junkie's dream!*

MRS. POWERS
*Surrealist nightmares with no place for decisions
in a country that's all prophets, look, someone
must quit prophesying
and for just once
mix Jerusalem's mortar and build the roof beam.*

DEACON DOXY
*Don't tell me about Eden,
I've got work to do.
Don't tell me about some drug-induced heaven.
The heaven I'm building
is three meals a day,
a roof over their heads—*

CHORUS
*And we're trying to build it for them and for you . . .
for you!*

(DOLLY *cuts the ribbon. All strike a photographic pose*)
(*Blackout*)

SCENE 5

An empty stage. A single spotlight on RUDE BWOY. *He addresses the audience.*

RUDE BWOY

>And Doxy, that John Crow fly all the way
>to the Big Apple, with a contract in him beak
>to bribe me for the opening of this lounge right here.

(DOXY *enters*)

DEACON DOXY

>There's no choice, Mr. Dawson. It's you or them.
>If there's going to be a lounge, there's
>got to be a hotel. If there's going to be
>a hotel, they'll have to go. What's wrong?
>>(*Pause. In the background, the* RASTAFARI *are beginning their exodus from the settlement*)
>
>It's a very good contract. Let's shake and sign.
>NATIVE SON RETURNS TO HIS ROOTS. Come on,
>this isn't the Club Number One, son.
>>(RUDE BWOY *signs the contract*)
>
>A copy for you. A copy for us. Shake.
>>(*Pause*)
>
>Try and imagine it. Right where you are
>could be the Babylon Lounge. Hear that applause:
>like the sound of the sea! You owe it to your fans!

(*Thunderous applause, whistles, etc.* DOXY *withdraws. Music.* RUDE BWOY *looks down at the contract he is holding*)

O BABYLON! Act 2 / Scene 5

RUDE BWOY
>   (Sings)
>   *I get a hollow feeling, now I've won.*
>   *I never thought that I*
>   *would envy Aaron,*
>   *one man to stand alone*
>   *against all Babylon,*
>   *lose everything him own*
>   *and still stay strong as stone;*
>   *that calls for more admiration*
>   *than my own.*
>   *But I'm a big black star,*
>   *a big, black star.*

(RASTARI WOMEN, led by VIRGIE, enter. Above them: Garvey's Black Star)

RASTARI WOMEN
>   *A big, black star.*

(Behind RUDE BWOY, the exodus begins . . . PRISCILLA watching them)

VIRGIE
>   (Sings)
>   *By the rivers of Babylon, we sat down*
>   *and wept.*

RUDE BWOY
>   Well, of course, all them squatters then—

CHORUS
>   *Sat down, sat down and wept.*

RUDE BWOY
> Like the old Jews had to move on.
> For the higher the towers of Babylon rise—

VIRGIE
> *Yea, we wept when we—*

RUDE BWOY
> The smaller man come—

CHORUS
> *When we remembered Zion—*

RUDE BWOY
> The bigger his lies—

CHORUS
> *Zion—*

RUDE BWOY
> Thy kingdom come, condominium—

VIRGIE
> *We hanged our harps upon the willows—*

RUDE BWOY
> Bulldozers start to break earth—

CHORUS
> *The weeping willows—*

RUDE BWOY
>Steam shovels start to eat grass,
>like prehistoric monsters making new history—

VIRGIE
>*For there, they that carried us away—*

RUDE BWOY
>New Zion coming—

CHORUS
>*Carried us away—*

VIRGIE
>*Captive!*

CHORUS
>*Captive!*

RUDE BWOY
>Old Zion pass—
>>(*Sings*)
>
>*Required of Rude Bwoy Dawson a song—*

CHORUS
>*Required of him a song—*

RUDE BWOY
>*Which same song he now sings,*
>*as his memory takes wings*
>*back to him as a boy*
>*in the days of his dread—*

Act 2 / Scene 5

RUDE BWOY and CHORUS
> *In the days of his joy!*

RUDE BWOY
> (Shouts)
> Forgive me, you all, forgive Rude Bwoy!
> When you alone, you is nowhere!
>   (Music)
>   (Sings)
> *Where reggae come from?*
> *Where my music was born?*
> *You will know is a dread song,*
> *grow your Abyssinian hair long,*
> *is here my music come from,*
> *reggae born in a back yard,*
> *jukebox playing back hard,*
> *from the corner sound-system,*
> *find the poor and it's found then.*

CHORUS
> *That's where reggae come from!*

RUDE BWOY
> *Where reggae come from?*
> *Is the bass that is played*
> *day and night by parade*
> *way down in west Kingston,*
> *in Dunghill and Trench Town.*
> *Reggae born in dark places*
> *by the light of the jukebox,*
> *bright red on black faces,*
> *that's where reggae come from.*

Where reggae come from?
From fighting oppressor
in Babylon, bruk them!
From Emperor Selassie,
mock him and you mock them!
That's where reggae come from.
Say a man come from prison
and find him woman gone,
that's one of many reason
why reggae was born.
Why reggae was born—

CHORUS
Why reggae was born.

SCENE 6

Rhythm under. Dusk. The shack partially demolished. PRISCILLA, *dressed to leave, with her plants, a suitcase. She paces, convincing herself.* RUDE BWOY *sits apart, watching. The rest of the settlement are still moving out.*

PRISCILLA
Him call me Whore of Babylon once, right?
Him swear to me him had change, right?
Me was carrying his child, and him beat me.
Look at them lights there, look how nice
the bright lights of Babylon look . . .
Come on, get bright, Miss Electric Gyal!

How we will live? How we will eat?
Go, girl. Go back to your old life.
Go, because . . .
   (Music)
   (Sings)
What dem have in Babylon
you cyan't get in Trench Town.
You were right, Rude Bwoy,
you were right.

Me missing all de happy times,
and I forgot the sound
of laughter, Sailor Bwoy,
where you sleep tonight?

Bring the sailor a beer.
His ship leaving quite soon,
my happy times in Babylon
is now my hard times here.

You were right, Rude Bwoy,
you were right.
Life short, spread a lickle joy
before them blow out your light.
What them have in Babylon,
dem don't have in Trench Town.
You were right, Rude Bwoy,
you were right.
What dem have in Babylon,
you can't get in Trench Town.
   (She dances)
Come, barman, bring another round.

*We are spreading joy tonight.
You were right, Rude Bwoy,
you were right.
What them have in Babylon
dem don't have in Trench Town.*

(AARON *comes into the yard*)

AARON
Priscilla . . . So them win, then?
(*She turns. He removes his tam. His head is shaven*)
Same as Samuel, eh?

PRISCILLA
Lord, Aaron . . .

AARON
(*Looking around*)
Is only hair, girl. It will grow back again.
Dem mash up this place good. Anybody leave still?

PRISCILLA
Dem going up a' Pinnacle to build again. See there.

AARON
And the carving? Who have the carving?

PRISCILLA
Samuel carrying it like the Ark of the Covenant.

AARON
Them wait all this time, till I come out?

Act 2 / Scene 6   O BABYLON!

PRISCILLA

>Yes. And me wait here to tell you. I'm going.
>Back to my parish, where the ground is good.
>And I can raise the child.

AARON

>Whether you go or not. Mek me ask one t'ing:
>Whatever I do, girl, pain make me do.
>I understand if you want fe go.

PRISCILLA

>Poor Rufus. Selassie come, and
>Selassie gone. And you never see him.

AARON

>Me never see God neither. But Him exist.

PRISCILLA

>Dem had big procession, and him grant audience
>to Sufferer and them others. Now, look there!
>Behind that lickle cloud is where them going.
>On Samuel mountain.

AARON

>   What will you do then, girl?

PRISCILLA

>I am with you, Aaron. The two of us is one.
>Let we join them up at Pinnacle.
>   (*They embrace*)

(*Music*)

O BABYLON! Act 2 / Scene 6

AARON
(Sings)
Every day, when morning a' break—

CHORUS
(Offstage)
Babylon! Babylon!

(*They walk toward the mountain*)

AARON
And the sky is a fiery lake—

(*The Settlement descends to meet them*)

CHORUS
Babylon! Babylon!

AARON
Ethiopia, Ethiopia, we sufferers for your sake—

CHORUS
Babylon! Babylon!

(*A march of greeting and triumph from the Settlement as they ascend the mountain*)

AARON
O Zion, come through the cloud, Deliverer—

CHORUS
Lift up the heart of the sufferer—

AARON

Show me the face of my Emperor
and plant my soul in Africa!

CHORUS

Babylon! Babylon!

AARON

And one day the lion shall lie with the lamb.
And I, in Zion meet the great I Am—

CHORUS

Babylon! Babylon!

AARON

On that fresh, fresh morning,
that smell of grass!

CHORUS

O bright Ethiopia, O Holy Ras!

AARON

Babylon, take warning,
it shall come to pass!

CHORUS

It must come to pass!

AARON

And every day when sun a' sink—

CHORUS

Babylon! Babylon!

O BABYLON!   Act 2 / Scene 6

AARON
With nothing to eat and sorrow to drink—

CHORUS
Babylon! Babylon!

AARON
I tell my kindred, even dread shall die,
it is written and said that the great I
Am shall be one with I,
shall be one with I.

CHORUS
Shall be one with,
shall be one with I!

AARON
I-and-I-and-I-and-I
I-and-I-and-I-and-I

CHORUS
Zion a' come,
Zion a' come someday,
Zion, Zion,
Zion, Zion,
Zion a' come someday.
Zion a' come!

(Exaltation. Their vision of glorious Zion)